Better Homes and Gardens®

step-by-step

yard & garden
projects

RJ 925369
93 87 81 111

Better Homes and Gardens® Books
Des Moines, Iowa

Better Homes and Gardens® Books
An imprint of Meredith® Books

Step-by-Step Yard & Garden Projects
Writers: Eleanore Lewis, Julie Martens
Editor: Kate Carter Frederick
Project Manager: Beth Ann Edwards
Art Director: Lyne Neymeyer
Photo Coordinator: Lois Sutherland
Copy Chief: Terri Fredrickson
Copy and Production Editor: Victoria Forlini
Editorial Operations Manager: Karen Schirm
Managers, Book Production: Pam Kvitne, Marjorie J. Schenkelberg
Copy Editor: Barbara Feller-Roth
Proofreaders: Holly Gilliland, Beth Lastine, Barbara Stokes
Contributing Technical Editor: David Haupert
Illustrator: Tom Rosborough
Indexer: Deborah L. Baier
Inputters: Janet Anderson, Connie Webb
Electronic Production Coordinator: Paula Forest
Editorial and Design Assistants: Mary Lee Gavin, Karen McFadden, Kathy Stevens

Meredith® Books
Publisher and Editor in Chief: James D. Blume
Design Director: Matt Strelecki
Managing Editor: Gregory H. Kayko
Executive Editor, Home Improvement and Gardening: Benjamin W. Allen
Executive Editor, Gardening: Michael McKinley

Director, Operations: George A. Susral
Director, Production: Douglas M. Johnston

Vice President and General Manager: Douglas J. Guendel

Better Homes and Gardens® **Magazine**
Editor in Chief: Karol DeWulf Nickell
Deputy Editor, Gardens and Outdoor Living: Mark Kane

Meredith Publishing Group
President, Publishing Group: Stephen M. Lacy
Vice President-Publishing Director: Bob Mate

Meredith Corporation
Chairman and Chief Executive Officer: William T. Kerr

Chairman of the Executive Committee: E. T. Meredith III

Cover photograph: Barbara Martin

All of us at Better Homes and Gardens® Books are dedicated to providing you with information and ideas to enhance your home and garden. We welcome your comments and suggestions. Write to us at: Better Homes and Gardens Books, Garden Editorial Department, 1716 Locust St., Des Moines, IA 50309-3023.

If you would like to purchase any of our gardening, cooking, crafts, home improvement, or home decorating and design books, check wherever quality books are sold. Or visit us at bhgbooks.com

step-by-step
yard & garden
projects

from the ground up

Ask yourself simple questions guaranteed to give you solid direction in creating the most satisfying outdoor areas possible. What works and what doesn't work in the current scheme? (For instance, mature trees provide essential shade and shelter, but a gazebo would add an attractive focal point and a room for alfresco meals; an existing patio would make an ideal outdoor getaway.) What problems need to be resolved? (Perhaps you need a place to store garden gear and outdoor furniture, or the garden lacks structural elements.) What do you want to do in your garden? (Think about all the ways that a dining area with a fire pit would enable you to entertain guests and have family picnics. Imagine having a place for moonlit baths framed by fragrant plants.)

plan ahead Just like a floor plan for a home, a garden design flows together and the various areas have logical locations. By connecting areas with meandering paths, you help ensure the flow. Mark entrances in style, with an arbor, a change in surface underfoot, or a door. Situate a potting area where all the needs of a gardening day, from tools to watering cans and soil amendments, are handy.

Where do you begin your garden projects? Start the adventure here. On the following pages, you'll gather plenty of ideas and inspiration to help you through the process. Use the tips and plans to make as many additions to your garden as your dreams allow.
first things first Before you break ground and dig into any project, take inventory. Consider your garden's existing features.

getting started

garden artistry

To decorate your garden, combine beauty and practicality. When adding decor to your garden, ask yourself two questions. First: "Is it me?" Select accessories that reflect your personal style and tastes. Add elements that you adore, not just those that you think will look good or happen to be on sale. A ho-hum garden overflows with unrelated items. An inviting garden emanates personality when it features a theme that's taken years to create, a one-of-a-kind sculpture acquired on a memorable trip, or a favorite color that's repeated throughout.

Second: "Do the decorative elements serve other purposes?" Dressing up the functional aspects of a garden, from paths and edges to plant supports and containers, boosts a garden's effectiveness visually as well as practically.

plan for change

Aim for artful simplicity. The larger the piece, whether art or furnishing, the more impact it will have. Adding lots of small pieces may result in a cluttered look.

Remember that outdoor decor fades, weathers, and deteriorates over time. Change is inevitable in the garden, in the accessories as well as in the plantings. Honor that natural process by incorporating art that's versatile, changeable, and movable. But first make sure your furnishings are the most well-made and long-lasting ones that your budget allows.

fancy flight

right: **Turn ordinary steps into a potted garden with a collection of unusual containers and a few decorative elements. An earthy theme of terra-cotta and gray spherical shapes dominates this scene. Pots and pedestals create additional layers of interest.**

Whether you're planning a new garden or scrutinizing an existing one, think about safety and convenience. For instance, can you stroll your garden paths without stumbling, even in the dark? Does your outdoor furniture store easily and require little upkeep? Could cushions make your garden more comfortable?

Perhaps it's time to update your garden by trading the railroad ties that frame planting areas for interlocking stone, or swap that old whirlpool bath for a low-maintenance fountain.

do yourself proud

Trade your trowel for a hammer or paintbrush and see what kind of garden decor comes to life beneath your hands. Throughout this book, you'll discover project after project for your garden, including wonderfully doable ideas, from fences and stepping-stones to seating and plant supports.

Each project features a complete materials list, as well as a quick-glance summary of the time and skill required. Also included with many of the projects is a cost guide, indicated by dollar signs. A "$" indicates that the project can be built for $50 or less. Projects costing $51–$100 are "$$"; projects costing more than $100 are indicated with "$$$."

Follow our plans step-by-step or use them as a springboard for your own creations. Making some of the items to decorate your garden will enhance your sense of pride and satisfaction.

cast in concrete
above: Take advantage of concrete's versatility by using it to anchor your garden's artful ambience. In this scene, hand-cast concrete art adds weatherproof form and sturdy substance with leaf sculpture and classic columns.

candle chandelier
left: Hang heavy items, such as a wrought-iron chandelier, from hardware designed to bear the weight. Keep candle flames well away from overhanging branches and other combustibles.

defining rooms

expand your borders

Garden rooms extend living areas beyond the walls of a house, spilling the stuff of everyday indoor life into the surrounding green space. With the price of land continuing to skyrocket and the size of lots shrinking, a yard counts as premium living space. If you have a yard, why not transform it into a place you yearn to be, sit, work, eat, sleep, interact, and find solitude?

Create a room in your garden or divide your yard into a series of rooms that fulfill all of these needs and more. The process is easy. Begin by choosing a place that lends itself to transformation. Add boundaries (shrubs, fences, walls) and you'll achieve a sheltered, private room outdoors.

overhead artistry

above: A ceiling defines a room with ease. An umbrella covers this dining area, transforming it into a shaded room.

woodland ramblings

right: A garden folly captures the imagination as a secluded destination. Furnishings expand the folly's usefulness.

walls to rooms

Whereas walls and fences provide privacy, trees, hedges, and bermed flower beds offer a living framework for a room. Structures such as a gazebo, an arbor, or a pergola define a garden room instantly. A sense of enclosure separates the place from surrounding spaces and enhances its character.

Begin the process of embellishing your garden room by answering these questions: Do you enjoy dining outdoors? Do you need a shady, secluded spot for relaxing after work? Do you want a resort-style room, complete with a spa? Do your children or pets require space to play? Include everyone in your household when you prioritize needs and desires, then plan accordingly.

restful retreat

above: In open spaces, a wall added as background to a seating area clearly defines a room's boundaries. Depending on the effect you want, include open windows which allow breezes to move freely through the room, or add windowpanes to shelter the area.

something from nothing

left: A garden swing, enclosed with an arbor, provides a garden hideaway for engaging conversation or quiet contemplation. Lattice and a backdrop of shrubs bolster the level of privacy.

adding practicality

good garden bones

Whether you're breaking ground for a new garden or you're an old hand with a hoe, your garden can benefit from structural embellishments.

To establish the framework of a garden, start with floor and wall treatments. Choose surfaces for underfoot, such as grassy paths, gravel, or stepping-stones. If you already have a deck or patio, consider dressing it up with a painted area rug. Spiff up walls with trellises, either cloaked with vines or left bare to show their structural form.

Think about the entrances to your garden and outdoor living areas. Would an arbor or a gate help direct traffic and make the area more welcoming or private? Adding an arbor gives you an opportunity to grow the climbing fragrant rose you've always wanted.

living wallpaper

right: Spruce up walls with trellises and vines. Rely on simplicity by choosing a classic garden design icon, such as a picket fence.

finishing touches

right: Decorate an entry with charming statuary or potted plants set atop pillars. The gate welcomes visitors.

bird's-eye view

far right: Use a birdbath as a cool oasis for a potted plant. Set the pot on rocks so it doesn't sit directly in the water.

decor resources
Highlight the natural attributes of your garden as you devise your decorating plans. In wide-open spaces, wind art comes to life as breezes drift through. Mask neighborhood noise with a trickling fountain formed from cast-off garden hoses or with a tinkling wind chime made from dangling silverware. Transform a shady nook into a luxuriously cozy corner by adding cushioned chairs and candles. Do all this and more on a limited budget by working with things you already have.

classy corner
left: Decorative elements abound in this corner garden next to the house. A wall trellis, a window box, and a small pond with a waterfall combine with plants to make a pleasing setting.

planning & decorating

dreams come true

Cultivate a personal vision for your garden. Begin by surveying your yard and putting what you see onto paper. Use accurate measurements to draw the existing features of your lot (house, patio or deck, planting beds, trees, shrubs, walkways, and such) to scale. Lay tracing paper over the map and indicate site characteristics, such as sunlight, soil type, and wind exposure, to help you figure out plant choices later. You can even plan your garden online by visiting **www.bhg.com/ bkgarden**.

stencil artistry

above: Armed with colored pencils and a garden template, embellish a bird's-eye-view drawing of your yard with the components of your dreamscape by stenciling in plants, walkways, fencing, and more into the layout.

expert advice

right: Brainstorm ideas with a landscape designer, crafting a personalized yard plan to fit a specific budget and time frame. If you wish, ask the designer to supervise the construction phase of your landscape.

Match the dream components of your outdoor rooms to the natural attributes of your yard, such as a reflecting pond for an empty courtyard or entryway, or a family picnic and croquet area on an expanse of shaded lawn. On another piece of tracing paper, pencil in the rooms you'd like to add to your yard. Indicate access points and traffic flow patterns. Mentally walk through the areas, considering the interconnectedness of each room. Continually ask yourself if each room's placement and flow enhance outdoor living or if they make simple tasks, such as harvesting fresh herbs for dinner, a major expedition. Last, use a fresh paper overlay to draw the details (structures, plants, and decor) that personalize your plan. From this point, implement your plan or meet with a professional to garner help in bringing your sketch to life.

inch by inch

above: If you must work alone and need to anchor a tape measure to mark a straight line, slip a large nail through the end of the tape and push it into the ground.

planning & designing checklist

- Couple your design with a plan of action that includes a time frame. Stretch projects over time to keep costs down. Do the work yourself whenever possible to save money and increase your personal-pride investment in the yard.

- Compare prices. If any part of your project requires a contractor, secure itemized bids from at least two contractors and compare them line by line.

- Ask for a written guarantee of any contractor's work. Request proof of their liability insurance. Set start and finish dates for each project.

- Rescue and reuse materials from your current yard before you begin a remodel. Transplant shrubs and perennials into holding beds; then move hardscape pieces. Recycle chunks of an old concrete walk into a stacked retaining wall or stepping-stones.

- Think ahead when laying electrical or water lines. Include extra outlets and spigots to accommodate future yard improvements in areas that remain undeveloped.

- Always invest in soil amendments for planting beds. Add organic material (compost, rotted manure, and chopped leaves) by the truckload before you tuck the first plant into a bed. Great soil grows great plants.

site preparation

survey your area

First, assess the lay of your land, focusing on the pros and cons of your landscape. Note everything, from areas of shade to wind exposure, from a good sunset view to eyesores or wet areas where water collects. Note these aspects on the basic map you made of your yard (see page 14). Stand inside your home and gaze out the windows. What you do to your yard will affect the view from indoors. Make a list of the views you presently savor, along with ones you'd like to change.

Before you construct anything, have a firm understanding of local building codes, easements, and neighborhood covenants that may affect your property. Contact utility companies to determine the location of underground lines. Be present when a utilities worker marks the lines; make sure all labels are clear. Add these lines to your yard map.

drafter's delight

above: Use graph paper to draw your landscape to scale. Be sure to include underground utility lines on your sketch.

plant tapestry

right: Before planting, set perennials and shrubs, still in their nursery pots, into place on the prepared bed. Shift pots as necessary to create an artful arrangement and to accommodate spacing for mature plant size.

Survey your yard through the seasons and marry problem areas with solutions that match your garden room wish list. Does the western sun beat mercilessly on your family room all summer? Create shady areas with fruit trees that dish up garden-fresh fare for your family. Do spring rains create a seasonal swamp in your backyard? Address that soggy space with a water feature or moisture-loving plants.

geometry works
above: Symmetrical beds add a formal element to a suburban backyard. Use a structural feature, such as a tuteur *(shown)*, a fountain, or an oversized container, to play center stage in your backyard scene.

side-yard switch
left: Transform an ugly-duckling side yard of grass into a graceful-as-a-swan allée (a tree-lined walkway). Begin by removing turf; then set balled-and-burlapped trees into place. Choose trees that will grow more up than out, such as colonnaded apple trees, narrow upright junipers, or columnar hornbeams. You might mark one entry to your allée with an arch, and place a bench at the other end.

your garden style

Focus on style as you plan your garden projects and it's more likely you'll be satisfied with the resulting cohesive, comfortable scene.

celebrate style As you peruse the following pages and survey the various garden styles, note your reactions. Which gardens appeal to you the most and stir your enthusiasm and sense of comfort? Which styles would enhance your home and the existing elements of your landscape?

Gather ideas and inspiration from the gardens shown and think about each style's hallmarks, from classical symmetry to tropical lushness, from artistically colorful to naturally rustic. Each style weaves a scene that starts with a few thematic anchors, including significant choices of materials, structures, and furnishings. **bring it home** Your garden's style provides a decorative theme that ties together different parts of the landscape. Your design approach should also reflect your personality and lifestyle as you choose appropriate materials and set the framework in place.

Choose materials that fit your budget and your tastes, as well as functional needs for paths, edges, furnishings, and other garden elements. Select coverings for garden floors and walls as you would indoor counterparts, considering color, texture, durability, availability, and ease of construction.

Let maintenance requirements influence your selection of surfaces and structural elements throughout the garden. Concrete, for instance, proves long-lasting and easy to dress up. Combine it with locally quarried stone for more artful appeal. Recycle broken concrete pieces from an old walkway into a new wall.

where to begin

garden decor

A beautifully planted garden draws interest and inspires wonder. But a beautifully decorated garden includes other elements that blend with the plants to make a setting that's attractive and complete. The place exudes a sense of design as well as comfort and personality.

What's more, a well-decorated garden makes your outdoor spaces more useful and rewarding. By planning carefully and including certain elements, you minimize maintenance chores and maximize privacy. Even the smallest spaces benefit from embellishments, from a sparkling fountain or birdbath to a musical wind chime or comfy chair.

Begin your decorating adventure here. On the following pages, you'll gather plenty of ideas and inspiration to help you through the process.

simple touches

below: Everyday objects, such as pots and a bench, combine in a setting that epitomizes effective garden decoration.

First, contemplate your garden's style. This unifying principle creates cohesiveness between house and garden, plus it provides an outlet for personal expression. Explore the design approaches on the pages ahead and see which ones mesh with your style. At this point, look at the big picture and start to consider which decorating materials seem most appropriate for your garden.

If you need more inspiration for designing your garden after looking through the rest of this chapter, visit **www.bhg.com/bkgarden** to find more information about garden design and projects.

structures unify
above: Use architectural elements, such as window-framing trellises, to unite house and garden. Upright structures also provide growing room for plants.

favorite things
left: Add a comfortable chair, a sturdy table, and a quirky accent to a quiet corner, and voilà! What better place to sit and read, savor homegrown tomatoes, or listen to the birds sing?

classic

timeless looks

Classic garden design never goes out of style. Ordered and refined, the look is typically formal. Sharp, uncluttered lines help define garden spaces. Architectural elements play a major role in defining the classic style, from elaborate gazebos and stately columns to simple but elegant urns. Gardeners position focal points, such as statues, structures, and pots, purposefully throughout the classic garden to draw eyes and wandering feet.

gorgeous gazebo

right: A stately garden house fits a small garden with ease. The open latticework allows surrounding plantings to show through. Flanking the entrance, a pair of tuteurs (pyramid trellises) represents a time-honored element in garden design.

grand entrance

left: Separate garden rooms with simple and stylish paths. Classical urns perched atop pedestals add eye-catching height to a garden. Planters reflect the seasons, playing garden-room sentries when filled with pansies in spring, ferns or impatiens in summer, ornamental cabbages in fall, and decorative greens and berried twigs in winter.

aged to perfection

Architectural elements, such as ornate containers, trellises, pergolas, and statuary, add character to a classic garden. Over time, they develop a rich patina that makes them look as if they had been rooted in the earth for generations. Transform gleaming new treasures for your garden into weathered beauties with these easy tricks:

- For concrete pots, wipe off the new and rub on the old by coating surfaces with black wax (ordinarily used on antiques).
- A mossy veneer is the understatement of established, ageless beauty. To seed moss onto concrete, terra-cotta, or brick, swirl a small handful of moss in a blender with buttermilk. Brush the buttermilk on surfaces to be mossed; then keep them shaded and moist. Moss will grow in seven to 10 days. Water brick walkways regularly to keep moss healthy.
- If you're adding a wooden structure, wipe freshly painted, still wet surfaces with a damp rag to create an instant weathered finish. Experiment to create the look you want.
- In outdoor seating areas, cover pillows with vintage fabrics that match your garden's well-seasoned ambience.

classic

design basics

A garden that revolves around classic design unfolds with the precision of a symphony. Whether in one area or between rooms, focal points draw the eye through the garden, from strategically placed structures to statuary or containers. A seamless blend of beautifully tailored lines clothed in lush plantings with few color changes epitomizes this traditional style.

The functional parts of a classic garden include pathways, structures, benches, and containers. Choose materials for these elements on the basis of their durability, versatility, and architectural capacity. Concrete offers all these qualities. When laying paths and purchasing containers, choose concrete for all-weather wear year after year. It stands up to the elements with ease. Allow concrete or cast-iron containers to sit outside through the toughest winter weather and replant them in spring. However, move terra-cotta pots, which are vulnerable to frost damage, indoors or into a protected shelter in regions where temperatures dip below freezing.

Metal trellises, furniture, and other pieces also stand up to harsh winters. Select weather-resistant wooden furniture made from teak or shorea (similar to teak but less expensive) for lasting enjoyment. If wooden structures remain in place through cold, wet weather, check them each spring for weak spots or wear, and make necessary repairs.

posy-lined path

right: **A strong framework is one key to a classic look. This concrete path provides an avenue, or allée, leading to spacious stepping-stones nestled in pea gravel. Striking structures pair handsomely with plantings. Subtle blooms and minimal color give the garden a cool, restful feel.**

On the softer side, use plantings as focal points. Tuck formal pedestal planters into a tangle of greenery. Manicure shrubs into neat shapes. In a tiny garden, place a graceful rose or a butterfly bush beneath a metal arch, creating a blooming focal point at the back of a planting bed or patio. In a larger garden, anchor a border planting with a weeping cypress or a tidy spruce, drawing the eye and suggesting the sense of permanence that a classic garden offers.

living room luxury
left: The refined lines of an iron table, a bench, and chairs transform a patio into an elegant retreat. A brick surface with moss filling in the cracks looks venerable and established. Frequent watering keeps the green carpet lush.

parterre garden
left: Symmetry represents a cornerstone of the classic look, rendered beautifully in a parterre design. This specialty garden features plants arranged in geometric patterns to create a sense of order. Boxwood suits a parterre, but if it is marginally hardy in your area, choose 'Northern Beauty' Japanese holly or dwarf balsam fir instead.

eclectic

choices, choices

Most gardens boast something of an eclectic style. A mix of elements, acquired from different places over time, comes together in the garden and may or may not work as a unified design scheme. The eclectic garden appears carefree and personal, conjuring a welcoming charm in its assortment of accessories, whether new, homemade, or hand-me-down.

If you make wise choices and present the elements of your eclectic garden with confidence, it's likely to work effectively as a whole. With a careful eye for composition and unity, you can happily

collector's garden

right: **A flea-market bench (repainted green and rubbed with a blue top coat), handmade ceramic and tile mosaic pieces, and mariposa slate stepping-stones from a builder's supply store unify this setting.**

include garage-sale goodies, as well as new features, to create a one-of-a-kind retreat.

Although all garden design entails a journey of choices, the eclectic garden allows you to combine various styles, from classic to contemporary, in a single scheme. Repeated materials, such as stone, tile, or galvanized metals, work as unifying elements.

In addition, choose a dominant color, and weave it throughout the garden using plants, paving materials, and assorted accessories. Paint furniture, details, and structures, such as birdhouses, to tie together your color scheme. Use paint or stain to make new items look old.

garden art
above left: **This windmill was a flea-market find at $65. The old watering cans make functional art; they're handy when the plants need watering.**

make a deal

Unleash your creativity to find good deals and decorate on a shoestring. Use these tips for bagging bargains:

- Arrive at garage sales and flea markets as early as possible.
- Go to auctions or tag sales on a weekday, when they're less crowded.
- When you find something that suits your fancy, negotiate a price.
- If you can't repair a rickety piece, plant flowers in it instead.

rustic

back to nature

Constructing rustic, one-of-a-kind structures transforms castoffs of the natural world (scrap logs, branches, tree prunings, driftwood, and weedy tree saplings) into artful, functional forms. Any gardener can master this art.

Acquiring the wood is easy. Seek local sources of native wood. Forage beaches or riverbanks for driftwood. Visit a construction site and ask the contractor if you can haul away cuttings. Scour curbs after heavy windstorms or traipse wooded areas for fallen branches. If asked, utility or tree service crews will also leave cuttings free for the taking.

willowy escape

right: **Elaborate and elegant, this willow bentwood structure offers welcome shade on a sizzling summer afternoon. Decorated with white lights, it makes a romantic getaway for candlelit dinners.**

best woods for bentwood

The choicest woods for outdoor structures stand up to several seasons of blustery storms, blistering heat, and blizzardy tempests. Long-lasting woods include cedar, juniper, arborvitae, bamboo, second-growth willow, and several kinds of locust. Woods with a shorter life span (one or two seasons) include elm, wild cherry, Oriental bittersweet, mulberry, mimosa, second-growth sycamore, ash, wisteria, and cottonwood. Grapevine also works well for outdoor structures, especially trellises or fencing, but it lasts only a season or two. Its naturally twisting growth habit can make it difficult to manipulate.

please fence me in

above: The tidy all-American picket fence takes a rustic turn when made with black locust trimmings. Drywall nails hold the pickets in place. Cut pickets so they stand clear of the ground, preventing moisture from seeping into the wood and causing rot.

rustic

tricks of the trade

Crafting rough, raw twigs and timber into stunning
structures requires nothing more than imagination,
a pile of wood, and a hammer and nails. Weaving
wood together creates wonderful structures that
appear to be rooted in place and part of the
natural landscape.

   Begin by seeing wood as a natural art form.
Let each limb inspire your design; fit together the
topsy-turvy angles and curves into strong, simple
joints. A soft crook in a branch becomes a peak

the view from here

right: **To whet your appetite for woodworking,
tackle small projects that give you a chance
to hone your carpentry skills. Build a twig
window box planter with a plastic window box
liner. The liner helps prevent early decay of the
wood and holds moisture for the plants.**

branched passage

right: **This gate
would make Mother
Nature feel welcome.
Brackets crafted
from apple and plum
tree trimmings dress
up the driftwood
uprights. Fruit tree
prunings, tacked onto
a wooden frame, form
the gate.**

for a garden arch; a quirky V-shape twig provides a bracket for a corner joint.

Making arches and curved trellises or fencing requires pliable wood. Young wood is most flexible; bend wood as soon as possible after cutting it. If you wait more than two or three days, the wood will break instead of bend.

Attach twigs and branches with drywall nails. Use wire to reinforce nailed connections. Green wood dries and shrinks once it's cut, so tighten wires with pliers a few weeks after building your work of art.

hardwood haven

left: Red cedar and mountain laurel form a gazebo and bench that look as if they sprouted from the ground. Peel bark from logs and apply a liquid preservative to the wood if desired. Otherwise, bark falls off eventually.

romantic

love grows

Transform your garden into a fairy tale come true by filling it to overflowing with the accoutrements of romance: fragrant flowers, curving lines, and hidden corners.

As you plan your storybook hideaway, remember that the feel of romance thrives on what is unseen. Tuck a water feature into a shady secret garden area so it is heard before it is seen. Enhance the mystery of your garden by granting glimpses rather than spacious vistas. Reinforce the theme with latticework, and take advantage of low-hanging limbs and lush hedges to create peekaboo privacy. The effect should be neither

tie the knot

right: **Use creative touches in your garden. A dwarf mondo grass love knot, complete with bows, trails along this stone walk, where turf wouldn't thrive in the shady passage.**

contrived nor cutesy; instead aim for simple, charming, and captivating.

Typically, a romantic garden boasts an abundance of roses and old-fashioned flowers (sweet pea, dianthus, and stock) emanating their heady perfumes. Or a sedate green scheme of shrubbery, hostas, and groundcovers cushions a shady corner.

Romance is a state of mind, so choose decorative details that inspire a cozy feeling, such as low-voltage lighting or candlelight, soft cushions for snuggly seats, and water gently trickling from a pond or tabletop fountain.

great plants for a romantic garden

bleeding heart	lilac
clematis	love-in-a-mist
cosmos	oriental lily
daisy	oriental poppy
delphinium	peony
foxglove	rose
heliotrope	stock
hydrangea	sweet pea
jasmine	wisteria

table for two
above: Transform a quiet garden corner into an outdoor cafe. Choose comfortable, sturdy furniture to enhance dining pleasure. This tiny table for two and folding chairs suit the cozy space. A brick floor keeps feet clean, making this a perfect spot for intimate dining.

sweet mystery of love

Romance hinges on mood and the senses. Cater to eyes, ears, and nose with a garden that bursts with sense appeal. Plants that promise sensory experiences include velvety lamb's-ear, lusciously fragrant lilac or mockorange, and traditional love-me, love-me-not daisy. Papery-petal poppy and cranesbill geranium glimmer in sunlight. Modest violet and lily-of-the-valley suggest old-fashioned charm. Evening-scented stock and moonflower call to mind moonlit evenings.

Delight your eyes by establishing focal points as well as vistas in the garden. Place seating every 10 feet within any secluded nook. Focus on feeling when you select materials for flooring. Instead of using prickly bark mulch or jagged gravel underfoot, choose soft, treadable plants, including Scotch moss, blue star creeper, and Corsican mint, perfect for going barefoot. Curves, such as bed edges, fence tops, chair backs, and trellises, prove luxuriously alluring. Place them liberally throughout your garden.

enchanting entry

right: **A beckoning bower and intricate iron gate exude romantic style. Victorian-era metalwork, with its curves and curlicues, adds forget-me-not style to any garden setting. To create a similar scene, establish fragrant climbing roses with heady fragrances at the base of your garden's portico. Great climbers include 'Climbing New Dawn' and 'Dainty Bess' (shown), 'Zephirine Drouhin' (thornless), 'Blaze' (red), and 'Mermaid' (yellow; ideal for Southern gardens).**

flair for comfort

left: A backdrop of shrubbery helps create a private getaway. Use fluffy cushions in pretty prints to encourage visitors to rest and relax.

decorative trims

below: An eye for detail helps enhance a garden's ambience. White paint and detailed cutouts make this wren house a home.

nighttime escape

left: Evening strolls in this garden lead to a romantic spot, complete with twiglike steel chairs and a table. Grassy ribbons between flagstones stroke bare toes; flickering candlelight adds allure.

artistic

art in bloom

Tucking art into a living masterpiece of bud and bloom is easy. The basic rule: Use simple plantings in a simple color scheme.

Remember that the art should be a focal point. Choose plants that have foliage or flowers in tones complementary to (rather than competitive with) the artful element. Pair ferny foliage with blocky artistic elements. Plant soft-tone flowers in drifts of a single shade to skirt a colorful work of art.

When adding art to an existing garden bed, consider how plantings look through the seasons. A sculptural element that plays center stage in a spring perennial bed may be overgrown by midsummer.

Adequately anchor art objects destined as permanent parts of the garden. Move artwork into storage before cold weather arrives, if pieces need protection.

flying fish

above: Let your imagination—and your art—soar as you arrange your garden gallery. This metal fish-shape birdhouse perches high above a sea of *Tithonia* (Mexican sunflower). The pink shed accents this garden designer's artful approach.

towering fountain
left: Where space is limited, art does double duty. When possible, select art that blends function with fancy. This moss-topped pedestal serves as a fountain and as a focal point in the midst of container plantings. Water trickles down the pedestal to the pool below.

window dressing
below left: Simple plantings, like beautiful frames, help display garden art. Here, santolina topiaries perform perfectly in a plain metal window box. Metallic gold dry-brushed paint artfully tints and ties together the shutter cutouts and the window box.

rock around
below: Take advantage of the artistic nature of rocks. A flagstone cistern cover, when adorned with a creative swirl of smooth stones, becomes a garden centerpiece.

contemporary

no-fuss beauty

For gardeners who want high style with low maintenance, the contemporary look delivers both. You can maintain an elegant retreat with minimal care.

Plantings adorn the sophisticated sleekness of this contemporary garden (*right*) with hassle-free good looks. Mass plantings of a single beauty, such as ornamental grass, steal the show.

Materials for paths and patios display their durability in a neat, uptown look that needs only occasional sweeping or raking. Decorative details echo the uncluttered approach. A fountain, a privacy-providing arbor, and a modest clutch of pots represent sophisticated elements that personalize the contemporary garden with understated charm and unbeatable good taste.

grassy good looks

left: Ornamental grasses provide a nonstop show of color, motion, and sound. Their stamina keeps pace with the seasons, peaking from summer through winter. Care is a snap. Cut off dead plant parts in early spring, as new growth emerges. Divide clumps when they begin to wrestle for space.

surface savvy

below: For outdoor rooms near the house, choose easy-care floors instead of lush green lawns that require mowing, trimming, and other time-consuming chores. Use pavers or bricks in seating areas; combine concrete or brick flooring with gravel or crushed stone for pathways.

retire your mower

Maintaining a patch of emerald lawn might suggest suburbia at its best, but for gardeners who long to stop and smell the roses, the green grass of home isn't all it's cracked up to be. Consider various healthy alternatives to lawn that look good but take less time to maintain. Buffalograss, heathers, sedums, sempervivums, and creeping herbs all make excellent groundcovers. For nonplant options, try pea gravel or a combination of cobblestones or pavers, with gravel or low-growing plants in between.

tropical

tropical punch

Languish no more in the blasé, cookie-cutter lawn–shrub–tree landscape of suburban sprawl. Pump up your yard's volume with a touch of the tropics. Roll out a carpet of sensually textured plants, flaming tiki torches, and hot-pink flamingos. You'll feel as if you've been transported to a delightfully exotic jungle (and the sense of a permanent vacation). Hang up a hammock and take in the tropics.

How long you'll enjoy the bodacious blooms of tropical beauties depends on where you garden. In warmer climates (Zones 7 and 8), transplant the tropics into your garden for year-round enjoyment. If you live in a temperate region, corral the wildness of the rain forest in containers and move them indoors before winter's chill arrives.

Select a tall, imposing plant (either in an oversized pot or in the ground), such as bamboo, abutilon, mimosa, or banana, for your sizzling paradise. Fill in around your selection with plants in a variety of textures, shapes, and colors. Cultivate an overgrown look by planting closely. Give houseplants an outdoor adventure by tucking them into your tropical landscape. The dramatic leaves of spider plant, purple setcreasea, and variegated snake plant provide bold color. The wonderful calypso look of crotons and Hawaiian ti plant, the sensual flowers of princess flower and canna, along with the sculptural foliage of fatsia and bromeliad also deserve a place in your tropical scene.

untamed and unrestrained

left: The big, bold foliage of tropical plants demands equally flashy, substantial architectural partners. Recycled columns from a remodeling job resemble jungle-engulfed ruins when surrounded by cannas, bananas, and palms. A simple path in muted tones complements the textural tapestry of leaves.

great plants for a tropical garden

agapanthus	citrus trees
bamboo	elephant's ear
banana	gardenia
bird of paradise	ginger
bleeding heart vine	hibiscus
bougainvillea	lantana
bromeliad	palm
brugmansia	plumeria
canna	princess flower

tropical

tropicalissimo

Fan the flame of the tropic's appeal by working touches of a vacation at the beach into your garden. A hammock or a hanging rattan chair will lull you into a world of tropical pleasure. Include pots of orchids around your deck or patio. The flowers linger lusciously. Clothe any patio paving surface with a simple sisal mat, which feels wonderful beneath bare feet. Keep an exotic bird, such as a parrot, in a caged perch. Set up outdoor speakers, protected under an eave or camouflaged inside lightweight rock-look casings, and crank up the calypso music.

unmasked jungle

right: Water splashing over rocks or dancing in a fountain adds to a feeling of tropical abandon. Lush plants camouflage pond edging and enhance this garden's tropical look.

furniture finesse

left: Select accessories that fit the flamboyant flair of the tropics. Long-lasting teak furniture can't be beat for weatherability; look for environmentally responsible plantation-harvested teak to preserve the rain forests. Shorea wood is as weather-resistant and durable as teak but costs substantially less.

tropical trickle

left: Small spaces revel in the luxury of water. Search out a dramatic container to make a musical water garden. A simple, bubbling fountain creates a tinkling melody. Orchestrate a series of bamboo water spouts in graduated sizes to play a symphony of running water. Good plants for containerized water gardens include houttuynia, iris, lysimachia, dwarf equisetum, and dwarf papyrus.

asian

garden refinement

Asian-style gardens comprise the universe in miniature. Stone, water, and trees represent mountains, oceans, and forests. Fluid lines compose natural-looking asymmetry.

Each part of the garden, from plants and surfaces to art, reflects thoughtful planning. Fastidious attention to building and maintenance results in a clean, groomed look.

Simple elements inspire an air of serenity through their careful selection and

eastward passage

right: **A shaded walkway becomes a path to Asia with the addition of a traditional multipiece stone Japanese lantern. The stepping-stones and the arbor form clean lines, typical of an Asian garden. The subtle color scheme of grays and greens speaks of tranquillity and peace.**

precise placement. This minimalist style lends itself to small spaces and limited time for maintenance.

The key features of Asian-style gardens take varied forms. Water trickles from a bamboo spout or reflects the sky in a still pond. Rocks appear as carefully placed boulders, selected for their artistry, set alone or as meticulously arranged groups.

Asian style emphasizes plant form and shape. Color schemes do not march through the seasons in brassy hues, but instead tiptoe along in subtle shades of green and gray. Occasional blooms or autumn foliage splash bright spots of color into the garden. Favorite plants include rhododendron, azalea, and Japanese maple. These species exhibit strong branch lines and welcome artful pruning. Flowering fruit trees, bowing ornamental grasses, and ferns are other classic plant choices.

set the mood
left: **For simplicity, bamboo excels. This bamboo gate, tucked in the middle of a white plank fence, proclaims this garden's Asian theme.**

altogether asian
left: **You don't need large spaces to craft a quintessential Asian garden, because attention to detail seals the style. Stone plaques, a latticework screen, and iron chairs set the stage for this garden. A bonsai tree, a tea set, and thoughtfully placed round rocks whisper of the Far East. Potted plants, including Japanese maple, bamboo, hostas, ferns, and feathery astilbes, enhance the setting.**

45

asian

beautiful bamboo

One of the strongest building materials around, bamboo includes a large group of fast-growing, graceful and drought-tolerant plants with varied landscape utility.

From short to tall, light to dark, and tender to hardy, bamboo offers variety to bridge every gardening gap. Black bamboo (*Phyllostachys nigra*) and green sulcus bamboo (*Phyllostachys aureosulcata* 'Spectabilis') are winter-hardy, towering giants. *Fastuosa* varieties, planted 3 to 5 feet apart, form a living screen in three years. For striking variegation, try dwarf *sasaella* bamboo.

versatile display

right: Bamboo works hard in this garden. Split and whole bamboo form the fence. A bamboo waterspout sings a playful tune in a stone basin, flanked by a clump of yellow-green bamboo *(Pleioblastus viridistriatus).*

bamboozled!

Look before you leap into growing bamboo. Plants spread by underground stems called rhizomes; running varieties spread more aggressively than clumping varieties. Use bamboo for erosion control or to make a living fence. Plant bamboo where it has room to grow, or keep it in a container.

To curtail bamboo's wandering ways, sink a plastic, barrier-type container (which should be available at the same place you bought the bamboo) into the soil surrounding the roots when you plant the bamboo. Leave 1 to 2 inches of the barrier above the soil line. Fill in with soil, then add 4 to 6 inches of mulch.

Use cut bamboo canes liberally in your garden. Tie canes to stakes or tepee-type plant supports, using twine. To connect and secure canes to fencing, gates, and other structures, use weather-resistant black polypropylene ties.

neo-traditional view
above: This garden blends Old World and new into a scene of sculptural beauty with its rose-covered arbor and traditional Japanese *koetsu-gaki* bamboo fence. Bamboo's long-lasting nature makes it an excellent choice for posts and fencing. Strong as steel, the canes' hard outer coverings repel water and resist rot.

all-together

piecemeal peace

The all-together garden blends choice features in a custom-look space that appears to have been carefully created all at once. But the greatest advantage of the all-together style comes by adding items over time as your budget and energy allow. The secret lies in gathering goods with a common theme, such as a material, color, or pattern. Provide seating the first season, a wall treatment the next season, and some floor decor for the third. As long as you follow the theme approach, any addition will fit into the garden.

For a budget-wise, finished-look garden from the start, focus on outfitting one small area at a time from top to bottom. Complete a floor treatment (to create the grass-and-paver design, *right*, see page 74); then add a couple of comfortable seats and a table. A section of retired fencing forms an instant backdrop, and a few substantial accessories complete the lived-in look. Tucked into a cozy corner, this ensemble boasts charm and affordability with simple themes. As other sections of the garden join the decorative show, a quick coat of white paint and black-and-white-striped fabric unify the diverse features into a cohesive whole.

repeated themes
right: Repetition of colors (white and black) and pattern (stripes or strong vertical lines) tie together this and other areas of the garden.

lattice-back bench
above: A custom-made arch, featuring prefabricated lattice, transforms a bench into a garden retreat.

heavenly vision
left: Combine a classic garden icon, such as a concrete cherub, with boxwood and brick to create a formal look in any setting.

custom good looks

The appeal of an all-together decorative style is
that the garden grows with you; its decor keeps
pace with your own changing tastes and budget.
Many gardeners follow a collect-and-blend
strategy that typifies an all-together look. Creating
a garden that's alluring and captivating requires
attention to detail as you tackle the hunting-and-
gathering phase.

How do you blend flea-market finds, tag-sale
treasures, and fresh-from-the-garden-shop
must-haves? Try a few tricks from some of the
top garden designers.

color Buy paint in your favorite color by the
gallon at your local home improvement center
so you can make furniture, containers, trellises,
birdhouses, and other accessories the same color.
This unifies divergent styles and types of furniture
and art.

fence finery
above: Repeat patterns of latticework
throughout a garden to blend separate areas,
such as planting beds and a garage wall,
into a seamless whole. In this scene, metal
fencing used to edge beds echoes and fits
the lattice theme.

potting bench
right: Include a work area in your garden.
A sturdy potting bench becomes a decorative
but practical work surface. This piece displays
a collection of antique terra-cotta pots on a
French wine rack.

fabric Add cushions to your garden seating. Use fabric in a single pattern to link chairs, benches, and other seating options that reflect different furnishing styles.

architecture Sprinkle traditional architectural shapes (spheres, diamonds, or arches) throughout a garden to marry planting beds and seating areas. Latticework, which is affordable and versatile, unifies a garden with charm.

collections Display your favorite whatnots throughout the garden. Large birdhouses, concrete planters, or wrought-iron pieces are some examples of popular collectibles.

seating for several
left: An extra-large bench is a real find. Watch for comparable specimens at antique sales and church auctions.

warm welcome
below: Dispense with the welcome mat when your front entryway includes inviting, cushioned, antique wire French furniture.

lay down the bones

The best landscapes provide private, shady hideaways as well as areas for entertaining and play. They balance a blend of expansive spaces and views with cloistered retreats for rest, reflection, and rejuvenation. They offer rooms for living outdoors: dining, sleeping, reading, and meditating. They include carefully placed decorative elements and the finishing touches of plants that weave a scene where you feel removed from the world, yet connected to it.

hardscaping helps The key to a successful landscape begins with its bones or hardscape. The portion of your landscape that is not green and growing, or the hardscape, includes walls, paths, steps, edging, patios, and decks. As you think about your garden space, mentally divide it into functional sections, such as planting beds, seating areas, and play areas for children or pets. Count on hardscape to delineate those separate areas of the garden.

A wall, for example, serves as a decorative and a practical element in the garden. A wall provides a sense of enclosure, forms a backdrop for plants, or turns unusable sloping ground into a livable terrace.

transforming spaces Weaving a unified tapestry of separate elements and spaces into a cohesive landscape relies on choosing the basic hardscaping components and threading them into the overall design with thoughtful planning. Once you've decided the place needs a wall to form an enclosure, for instance, you'll need to figure out where to place the wall, as well as what building materials would best suit the space and its uses.

Plants also serve diverse functions in a garden. Besides adding flourishes of beauty, they screen a view, enclose a bench, and supply living color. Trees, shrubs, flowers, and other plants make gardens infinitely more livable and enjoyable.

installing a garden

you will need

string, stakes, and powdered lime

wheelbarrow

compost, rotted manure, and gypsum

landscape fabric

bricks

herb plants

mulch: gravel, shredded bark, or cocoa bean hulls

rake

step-by-step

Bricks edge the simple geometric beds and make a neat peripheral path along this pretty parterre. Gravel paths between the beds make for easy access and maintenance. The open fencing provides a sense of enclosure and privacy, as well as a perfect support for roses, raspberries, and flowering vines. The design adapts to a smaller or larger space.

formal design

right: **Four triangular beds form the basic design for this 10×15-foot herb garden.**

lay path Plot the perimeter of the garden and the bisecting paths with string stretched between stakes. Use powdered lime to mark the beds and paths on the soil. Prepare the soil in the beds by amending it with several wheelbarrows full of compost, rotted manure, and chopped leaves. Dig or rototill to blend these amendments with powdered gypsum. Tamp down the soil in the paths to level them. **1**

edge with bricks Lay heavy-duty landscape fabric on the paths to deter the growth of weeds. Let the edges of the fabric extend far enough into the beds to set bricks or similar edging material on top of the cloth and hold it in place. Set bricks end to end around the edges of the beds. If you prefer, stand the bricks on their narrow side. **2**

plant Start with herbs or other plants in 3-inch to 1-gallon containers. The larger the plants, the sooner they will mature and fill the garden. Before unpotting, arrange the plants on the beds to determine where to position them. Unpot each plant and place it in the soil at the same level it grew in its nursery pot. After all the plants are in their beds, water them thoroughly. **3**

mulch Spread mulch at least 2 inches deep on the paths to finish the installation. Rake the surface to smooth and even it. Choose coarse gravel or finer pea gravel, shredded bark, or wood chips for soft pathways. Cocoa bean hulls make a chocolate-scented path but have a tendency to blow or wash away; combine the hulls with a heavier mulch to keep them in place. **4**

building a wall

cost	make it	skill
$$$	2-3 weekends	moderate

you will need

- stone
- stakes
- string
- level
- shovel
- gravel
- sledgehammer
- trowel
- chisel

stack 'em up

There's something timeless and enchanting about a stone wall. Whether it frames a garden room or a planting area, a stone wall has a rugged look that suits most gardens and adds a sense of permanence.

When planning a wall, consider its size, shape, and purpose. Enclosed by a wall, a garden room gains privacy, wind protection, and an attractive backdrop. A walled planting area, on the other hand, rises above ground level to define a room without blocking the view. A retaining wall refutes the claim of gravity on a hill, transforming unused sloping ground into terraced planting space. A knee-high wall proves moderately easy to build.

Learn about the types of building materials available in your area by visiting a landscaping retailer, building center, or stone yard. Bring along measurements and ask the staff to help you determine which types of stone or other materials suit your needs and budget. Flat stone makes the process easier; use interlocking stones (or modular masonry blocks), if you prefer. Save money by choosing a plentiful native stone or by building with techniques featuring concrete block, straw bale, or adobe.

enduringly yours
right: **A stacked-stone wall adds texture and scale to a garden. Flat, rectangular stone produces a tight fit and a sturdy wall.**

1 groundwork To build a dry-stack stone wall, purchase stone and underlayment (gravel) and arrange a delivery. Minimize hauling by having stone piled close to your work site. Lift with your legs and not with your back to avoid injury. Use stakes and string to mark the wall's course. Pull the string taut between the stakes, making sure it's level. Dig a shallow trench that's just below the frost line in your region; local building authorities can give you that measurement.

2 well grounded If you're working on a slope, cut the back side of the trench at an angle slanting into the slope. For drainage, line the trench with about an inch of gravel. Place the longest stones as the bottom layer. The fewer the joints in the first layer, the less chance of freeze-thaw cycles heaving your wall. Level stones as you lay them; tap stones with the handle end of a sledgehammer to settle them into place. Trowel soil beneath a wobbly stone to stabilize it. If you must cut a stone, use a sledgehammer and chisel.

3 stone upon stone Stack stones so that each stone bridges a joint in the row below it. If you're building a retaining wall on a slope, dig a hole into the slope every 4 to 6 feet and lay a long stone perpendicular to the wall, with one end resting on the wall and the rest of the stone extending into the hole. Use these same techniques whether you're building a straight or a curved wall. (Check local building codes and consider hiring a contractor to build a wall more than 3 feet tall.)

yard & garden projects | **57**

laying a floor

cost	make it	skill
$$-$$$	weekend	easy

you will need

- spray paint or flour
- spade
- road–grade gravel
- hand tamper or plate compactor
- builder's sand
- rake
- pavers
- diamond or wet saw
- rubber mallet
- broom

floored!

When considering a floor for a garden room, think beyond lawn. Although turf blends into any outdoor scene, hard surfaces offer decorative panache and durability.

Choose flooring for your garden rooms, and the paths that connect them, knowing that the surface must endure more than foot traffic and the vagaries of weather. Hardscape will also support heavy objects or items that require a level, solid surface, such as furniture, a grill, or a spa.

Use similar flooring materials throughout your garden to link diverse areas or rooms with a common design theme. Concrete, brick, and stone provide sturdy surfaces that last a lifetime. Brick pavers come in a variety of sizes, colors, and shapes that are easily adaptable to patios or paths. From cobbles to stepping-stone-size pavers, bricks offer design possibilities that conquer curves with ease and shape edging as well. Rent a diamond or wet saw to cut bricks.

wall-to-wall bricks

right: **Roll out your own garden-variety red carpet with red bricks. These kiln-dried pavers offer endless pattern variations and longtime persistence, bearing up well through seasonal extremes.**

1 **set the course** To construct a brick floor, such as this path that wraps around a wall, mark the floor's boundaries with spray paint or flour; then remove the sod. Use a spade to excavate the soil to a depth of 5 inches plus the thickness of your flooring material. Spread a 4-inch layer of road-grade gravel in the trench; tamp it down. For floors less than 80 square feet, compact the gravel using a hand tamper. For larger floors, rent a plate compactor.

2 **complete the floor** Build the wall (see page 56), then complete the floor. Add an inch of builder's sand to the floor, leveling it with the back of a rake. Set pavers on top of the sand, snugly against one another, in the desired pattern. Use a rubber mallet to tamp pavers into place. Spread a ½-inch layer of dry sand over the floor. Sweep it into the cracks between the pavers, then water the floor using a fine spray. If the floor feels wobbly over time, sweep in more sand.

stone smorgasbord

Crushed rock comes in many types and builds a floor that drains well and requires little maintenance other than occasional raking and replenishing. Visit a stone yard, quarry, or landscaping retailer to discover the range of alternatives. In general, a ton of crushed rock covers 90 to 100 square feet. Delivered from the quarry, crushed rock outbargains bagged rock mulch. Avoid loose stone as a floor treatment in areas frequented by rolling carts, high heels, or chairs that require movement, such as those around a dining table.

adding structure

structurally sound

Count on garden structures to frame spaces in your yard, creating sensible, tasteful subdivisions of the landscape. As focal points, structures punctuate a garden. Some structures provide overhead shelter, offering a dry place on a rainy day and a refreshing pool of shade on sweltering afternoons. Other structures define boundaries for your garden rooms and transform unused areas into your favorite gathering places.

aspire higher

right: **A corner trellis and storage benches add interest to an ordinary deck. The substantial posts, overhead lattice, and potted plants create a sense of sitting in a private, lushly planted garden. The bonuses: cushions, storage areas, and plenty of natural lighting.**

garden structure glossary

arbor: Arches or latticework; for vertical interest, supporting vines, and providing shade. Types of arbors reflect architectural styles, such as Arts and Crafts or modern.

folly: A garden house designed to offer scenic interest and protection from weather; originated in English estate gardens.

gazebo: An open, airy place that provides shelter and a view of the garden.

pergola: An open roof supported by columns or posts, covering a room or a walkway. Vines scramble across a pergola roof.

ramada: The Spanish word for arbor. Open-sided and sometimes attached to a building, a ramada has a solid roof (wood shingles, tile, or such).

trellis: This two-dimensional structure helps support and train climbing or vining plants and adds vertical interest to the garden.

Find inspiration for structural elements in classic architectural design motifs, famous historic gardens, and magazines. Keep a clipping file of ideas, making notes as you mentally translate them to suit the scale and style of your home.

Although the price of structural elements varies widely, prefabricated structures may cost more than ones you build yourself. Designing your own structure and hiring a professional to tackle construction are other options. Whatever method you choose, buy the best materials you can afford. Top-quality components cost more but last longer.

Before placing any structure in your garden, stand inside your home and visualize the feature in place. Make sure you'll enjoy the view from indoors as well as from various areas of the yard.

salvage style
above left: A garden folly mirrors a classic icon of Greco-Roman architecture: the rotunda. This retreat features an upended satellite-dish roof and beach-combed wharf piling posts.

walk this way
left: Arbored walkways lead you along a wooded path and provide resting spots. Fenced for safety on steep terrain, the arbors add structural interest.

adding plants

make room for greenery

Landscaping pays. Using plants to improve the aesthetics of your property increases its value. Properly positioned plants also reduce home heating and cooling costs.

But plants do more than put money in your pocket. They beautifully soften a scene and frame its outstanding features. Imagine the view in this cozy corner (*right*) without plants. Bricks and concrete would steal the show in a room that lacks definition and invitation. Add plants, and voilà! Hedges form walls that enhance privacy. Trimmed boxwood borders artfully echo the room's angular design. Colorful annuals delight the eye.

Include plants in your landscape plan (see page 14), indicating existing and new plantings, but wait to sink a trowel into soil until you have installed structures, walkways, irrigation lines, lighting, and such. Place hardscape first to avoid damaging plant roots with heavy equipment and digging. Stay away from existing trees and shrubs when using heavy machinery to avoid compacting the soil and injuring roots or stems. Avoid excavating deeply around trees.

Prepare planting beds according to soil needs of the flowers and shrubs you'll be adding. Your local extension service provides soil tests and suggests ways to address soil deficiencies. When planting, place the largest plants first. Imagine plants at their mature size and give them room to grow. Tight quarters require compact plants; choose dwarf varieties with smaller potential than their standard-size cousins.

For interactive planning help when adding plants, visit **www.bhg.com.bkplanagarden**.

top to bottom

right: **Mimic nature in your approach to landscaping by planting layers: trees overhead, shrubs from waist to head height, and groundcovers underfoot. Fill the spaces with perennials and annuals.**

Plan ahead for your plants' maintenance requirements too. If you don't have lots of time to tend the garden, choose native plants for easy-care beauty. Select drought-resistant, disease-resistant, and slow-growing varieties. Although annuals offer stunning, season-long color, they also require annual replacement, as their name suggests. If you garden where winter brings snow cover, include plants that stitch interest into a white-quilted landscape.

ideal plant deals

Make the most of your plant budget by following a few simple plant purchasing tricks:

- Shop with a list. Avoid impulse buying. Stick to your plan.

- Plant in spring and fall. Find the best selection, especially of perennials, early in the season. As spring turns to summer, look for bargains at seasonal garden centers, such as those at grocery stores.

- Predetermine which size pot you want and shop for plants on that basis. If you're planting a tree for shade, for example, start with the largest one your budget allows and enjoy the tree's shade in your lifetime. Buy perennials in the largest pots affordable for a more finished-looking garden. Use budget-friendly bedding plants as fill-ins.

- Purchase plants locally to save on shipping, but shop mail-order catalogs for an extensive selection and specials. Choose reputable plant purveyors that offer guarantees for replacement or money back.

plant shopping
above left: At the nursery or garden center, group plants as you might place them in your garden. Survey the collection with an eye for color and texture. Mix and match plants to please the eye and meet site requirements.

adding plants

plantscaping wisdom

Select plants to populate your garden rooms with color, fragrance, and a seasonally changing backdrop. Assess your planting space and surrounding living areas and decide if, for instance, you want plants for color, noise muffling, privacy, or shade. In cozy garden rooms, narrow planting beds often skirt the edges of the space, promising little room for roots. In this case, grow up. Use trellises, vines, wall planters, and hanging baskets to create a lush and beautiful view.

Containers eke out garden space in areas thick with hardscape. Choose pots with looks that rival the plants filling them, particularly if you have room for only a few containers. Use saucers to protect surfaces beneath pots. For accents, perch character-rich garden art sparingly among confined beds or a container garden. Avoid purchasing plants until you have a plan in hand, especially when filling lilliputian-size gardens. Otherwise, you may overbuy.

tight fix

above right: **Combine colorful flowers, wall-hugging vines, and hanging baskets to groom a garden that's short on space but long on looks.**

perennial pleasures

right: **In this walled garden, perennial plantings come and go with the seasons, lending themselves to up-close viewing to savor their beauty.**

potted gardens

left: Containers keep gardens going strong in rooms where cramped quarters prevent lavishly expansive planting beds. Arrange pots to add visual punch to a setting, clustering them in odd-numbered groups. Display showy ornamental containers by placing them at the center of attention: as sentries at the entrance of a room, flanking a seating area, or standing at the front edge of flower beds. Within the garden, elevate a large pot on a pedestal, on a tree stump, or on a concrete block.

underfoot, overhead & in between

Floors, walls, and ceilings represent a garden's essential boundaries. As you consider surfacing options, inventory the materials used currently in your yard. Add to the list any potential materials that suit your fancy as well as your plans. Mix materials according to your budget and the mood you wish to create. Combine one material with a less expensive one, such as stone with gravel. Keep in mind the long-term costs of maintenance, comparing care-free vinyl fencing with wood, which requires repainting, for example. Then think of all the possible ways to pair a wall, fence, floor, or ceiling with plants.

staying grounded In a well-crafted garden, flooring sprawls underfoot in myriad ways, from a lush carpet of lawn, to hardwood decking, to easy-care concrete, flagstone, or pavers. Paths connect outdoor areas and direct traffic; floors help define rooms and enhance their purposes.

what goes around When you add a wall, a fence, or a screen to your garden, use the structure to frame an entry, enhance privacy, or hide an unwanted view of garbage cans or utility meters.

If walls or a fence won't work into your design scheme, frame your garden with an overhead covering instead. A retractable awning or a leafy vine-clad canopy can define a garden space and change with the time of day or the seasons. The ultimate garden ceiling turns a classic architectural form, such as a wooden pergola, into a handsome growing space for flowering vines or climbing roses.

floors

paths and patios

Tending to a garden's floor transforms a lovely scene into a functionally fanciful environment.

It's best to tackle ground-covering treatments before planting. But adding paths through established lawns and gardens can be done. When trading lawn for walkways, select surfaces that dovetail dashing good looks with tough-as-nails durability. Bricks, pavers, gravel, and concrete top the most-wanted list of materials in landscaping circles.

Mix media to make paths and patios with one-of-a-kind looks at do-it-yourself prices. It's OK to blend bricks and gravel or recycled glass and concrete. It's also fun to pour concrete and

brick-a-brac

right: **Red and black bricks laid in an angular pattern create a dramatic patio. Use soldier-straight rows of bricks to contrast and delineate path and patio areas.**

abstract appeal

right: **Concrete strips poured between sections of concrete-and-stone aggregate yield a sculptural, easy-care floor.**

defined areas

far right: **An orderly framework of bricks lends a formal feel to a path. Plantings soften the hard edges.**

embed it with stones, tiles, or bits of broken china. Turn your creativity loose. Call in a contractor if you have an inordinately large area or a complex configuration, such as sharp turns or steep slopes.

Consider adding low-voltage lighting at the same time you lay garden floors (see page 255).

For help with more gardening tips and projects, visit **www.bhg.com/ bkgardenliving**.

squares and curves
left: Laying an outdoor floor doesn't have to be the swan song of your lawn. Square pavers make a neat curved path across a former area of lawn. Now grass and clay meld in a catchy rhythm.

floors: brick

cost	make it	skill
$$	2 days	easy

you will need

- stakes and string
- pickax
- spade
- landscape fabric
- gravel
- builder's sand
- plastic edging
- 10-inch–long steel spikes (⅜-inch diameter)
- bricks or pavers
- rubber mallet
- two 2×4s
- one 1×12
- heavy scrap boards and nails
- broom
- garden hose

brick island

Incorporate a hard-surface floor into a garden area to make an instant room. Flooring gives furniture firm footing as well. With a seating ensemble in place, your garden begs to host starlit suppers, morning coffee, and kick-back weekend brunches.

Bricks or concrete pavers promise patterns aplenty. Customize your patio with a personalized design. For your first project, choose a pattern that highlights the angular nature of bricks, laying them in straight or gently curving patterns (cutting bricks with a diamond or wet saw takes practice).

For the best brick bargain, locate clean, salvaged bricks, or you'll invest energy in chipping away clinging mortar. New brick pavers rank as moderately expensive among flooring options, but their durability justifies the cost.

dining in the round
right: **A brick floor forms an ideal basis for a garden room.**

1 define the edges To construct a brick patio, begin by defining the patio shape with stakes and string. Use a pickax and spade to excavate a 5-inch-deep base plus the thickness of a brick. Line the area with landscape fabric. Add and compact gravel to form a 4-inch base. Top gravel with 1 inch of builder's sand, leaving a slightly raised crown in the center of the area to allow for settling. Anchor plastic edging with steel spikes. Set border bricks into place.

2 lay the bricks Tamp sand with a handmade tamper fashioned by nailing heavy boards to the end of a 2×4. Begin to lay the bricks along an edge. Fit bricks together snugly; gently tamp them in place and level using a rubber mallet. As you work, kneel on a 1×12 board laid on top of the bricks to avoid disturbing the level bricks and sand base. Level disturbed sand, if necessary, using the edge of a 2×4. Keep the site covered with a tarp if it rains during construction.

3 finish the job Toss handfuls of builder's sand over the finished brick floor. Working from one side to the other, use a stiff broom to sweep sand over the bricks until the cracks are filled. Water with a fine mist from a garden hose. Repeat the process a week after construction and whenever bricks wobble.

yard & garden projects | **71**

floors: stained concrete

cost	make it	skill
$-$$$	weekend	easy

you will need

- concrete stain
- concrete cleaner
- scrub brush
- rubber gloves
- knee pads
- manual pump sprayer
- tarps or old sheets
- paintbrush (optional)
- sealant (optional)

concrete cover-up

If your dreams of a garden room include a spacious floor, concrete combines affordability with long-lasting durability in any climate. Use stain to soften concrete's harshness and create a warm look.

Concrete coloring options abound. For a soon-to-be-poured concrete area, purchase a powdered dye to mix into wet concrete. With this approach, as the masonry wears, newly exposed surfaces show a consistent color. If your concrete came with your home, blend the nondescript gray into surrounding plantings using an easy staining technique, such as the one shown *opposite*. Some stains involve acid etching, which initiates a chemical reaction between the staining solution and the concrete to fashion a colorfast surface. Other stains create a rich palette that mimics marble. Combining staining and etching techniques yields the look of cobblestone. Explore the options and browse color swatches at a local home improvement store or on the Internet before committing your concrete to one particular procedure.

color your world

right: Choose a concrete color that blends with surrounding plantings, structures, and furnishings. The concrete's terra-cotta tone complements the silver-blue of the table, chairs, and nearby foliage plants.

1 **choose a color** Concrete staining techniques work on individual pavers as well as on slabs. Stains may not hide concrete defects or discoloration, but cracks give the surface a weathered look. Remember that stains, like paint, appear darker when spread over a large area. Unify separate rooms by using hues in the same color family. Stain masonry surfaces (including upright ones) throughout your garden. Apply stain to existing surfaces or to new ones using the same techniques.

2 **clean the concrete** Water-base stain, which won't harm the environment, will adhere only to clean, dry concrete. Use a concrete cleaner, following the manufacturer's directions. Cleaning concrete requires nothing more than a scrub brush and old-fashioned elbow grease. Wear rubber gloves and knee pads for protection. Allow cleaned surfaces to dry thoroughly before staining them.

3 **begin to stain** Before you start staining, dab a little on an inconspicuous spot to check the effect. Use a manual pump sprayer to apply stain. Protect surrounding surfaces, including plants, from donning a new hue by covering them with tarps or old sheets. Apply as many coats of stain as the manufacturer suggests. If you stain steps or vertical elements, such as concrete columns, trade the pump for a paintbrush for better results. Apply a sealant if you wish.

floors: grass & pavers

cost	make it	skill
$$–$$$	weekend	easy

you will need

- square concrete pavers
- spade
- landscape fabric
- sharp digging spade
- plastic mesh grid (optional)
- rubber mallet
- sharp knife

garden parquetry

Ribbons of turf woven through a hardscape surface break up what could be a large expanse of concrete or other uninspired material. The design looks both finished and refined but it requires little expenditure and initial effort.

First, measure the size of the area and figure the square footage of your desired grass-and-paver floor. Calculate the grass area by laying a few pavers (of the size and type you desire) on a flat surface, such as an area of existing lawn, and determine the width of the grass intervals between the pavers. Plan for grass squares the same size as the pavers or for narrower stripes. Use those dimensions to estimate how many pavers and how much landscape fabric you will need for the entire area. Use a spade to excavate sod and soil to a depth that will place pavers even with surrounding lawn. Line excavations with landscape fabric. Set pavers in place and trim sod to fill any spaces. Keep the sod watered until it's established.

If you use this parquetry technique for a turnaround or an occasionally used parking area, lay a plastic mesh grid on top of the landscape fabric to provide extra support for the pavers.

elegance unveiled

right: **Capture the classic good looks of a formal garden with a grass-and-paver design. Mow the turf as you would an ordinary lawn.**

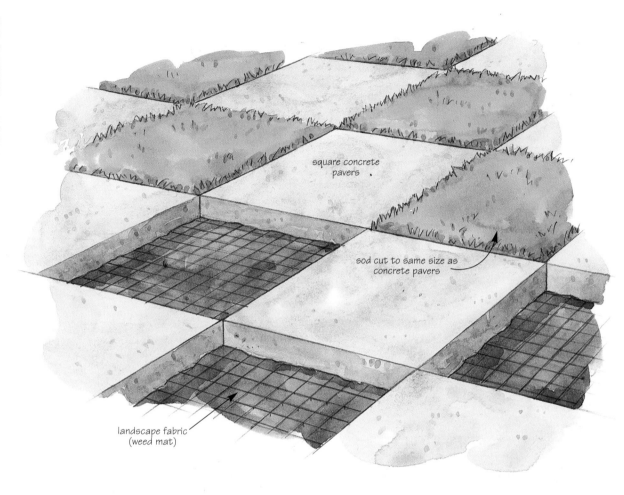

square concrete
pavers

sod cut to same size as
concrete pavers

landscape fabric
(weed mat)

harlequin lawn
above and *left:* In
a small new yard
(where grass has yet
to grow), you don't
have to sacrifice
green space in order
to include a patio.
Enjoy both by
installing a grass-and-
paver floor.

floors: mosaic

fancy footwork

When dreaming up your garden's good looks, keep in mind that what's beneath your feet can also dazzle the eye. A mosaic rug for the garden requires no more upkeep than an occasional brush with a broom or a splash with the hose, but it rakes in bushels of compliments.

Site your stone-embroidered carpet in a prominent place: beneath an entry arbor, between garden rooms, or skirting a prized focal point. To reap the greatest enjoyment from your ground-level artwork, position the mosaic where it's visible from second-floor windows. Draw or lay out your pattern to size before breaking ground.

magic carpet

right and *below:* **Gather your mosaic materials from local sources, such as building supply or garden centers. Use leftover hardscape materials from another garden project. This pebble-and-paver mosaic measures 48 inches square.**

paving materials

1. 3- to 5-inch river rock (100 pieces)
2. cobblestone
3. recycled clay street brick
4. Holland paver brick
5. Holland paver block
6. crescent Holland paver brick
7. handmade clay and mineral-glaze tile
8. peach and plum decorative lava rock
9. 1-inch recycled glass
10. interlocking paver

To build a rocky rug, excavate an area that's 2 inches bigger than the completed carpet. Remove sod and soil to a depth of 6 inches in frigid regions; 4 inches suffices for warmer climates. Lay crushed gravel (4 inches deep for cold zones, 2 inches for warm); top with 2 inches of sand. Snuggle stones and bricks into the sandy bed. Start with the largest piece. To center a paver in the heart of the rug, measure in from each corner. Work out to the edges of the mosaic, carefully positioning pieces.

Border the mosaic with cobblestone and brick, leaving a 3-inch edging frame. Fill in areas around stones with colored gravel and recycled glass. Increase stability by sprinkling sand or dry mortar mix over the finished carpet. Gently sweep the stabilizer into place, brushing away excess. Fill in the outside frame with soil; top with river rock. The mosaic will settle an inch or two over time.

step lively

left: Create a stepping-stone-size mosaic using a patterned concrete block. Excavate an area the same size as the block, adjusting depth until the block sits at soil level. Fill the block openings with soil, leaving an inch to top off with colorful recycled glass gravel.

walls

strong and silent

In the garden, walls create enclosure in one
area and enhance a sense of openness in another.
Place your walls strategically to shape a sanctuary.

Aim for privacy that's complete or partial,
depending on your needs. For example, a spa
or pool calls for a higher level of seclusion than
a play area or a dining room.

Position walls to separate an area but allow
accessibility. Before adding a wall, consider all views
extending to and from the proposed enclosure;
avoid blocking views.

Choose a good-neighbor wall design that
looks acceptable from either side, although both
sides need not appear the same. If the wall edges
your property, confirm the property line and any
easement restrictions before building. Determine
building code and permit requirements that may
affect the wall's height and construction method.

Avoid making a harsh, prisonlike wall by
adding elements of interest to it. Decorate the flat
surface of a wall using construction techniques,
such as a stucco treatment, tile inserts, carved
niches, or cutout windows. Incorporate a fountain,
lighting, or hanging planters when building
the wall, including the necessary hardware or
electrical elements in its construction.

wall flowers at work

right: **When building a stacked-stone wall,
tuck soil between rocks for plants that will
thrive there, including alpine varieties of
dianthus, armeria, draba, and sedum.**

sculptural detail

above: Embellish a stucco or adobe privacy wall with raised details. The chevron design, made by setting molds into the wall and covering them with stucco, is echoed in the wooden gate's construction.

flowery finesse

left: Garden walls offer excellent decorative potential. Fit your walls with a fountain, a birdbath, planters, or artful plaques.

79

walls: stacked stone

cost	make it	skill
$$$	3 weekends	moderate

you will need

- rope or garden hose
- spray paint or flour
- wooden stakes
- pencil
- string
- line level
- shovel
- flat stones
- sand

rock walls

A stacked-stone wall lends a distinguished air to even the youngest garden. The wall can be several feet high, although most dry-stacked walls (no mortar) run roughly 3 feet high, simply because it's hard to lift stones much higher than that. Most municipalities don't require permits for walls less than 3 feet high, but contact local authorities before breaking ground.

If you're building to 3 feet high, the wall's base width should be 2 feet. For higher walls, add 8 inches to the base width for each additional foot of height. Most dry-stacked walls withstand some freeze-thaw cycles, so this building technique works in all climates. Choose stone at a local quarry; have delivery personnel place the stone as close to your work site as possible to minimize lugging. Because this project is physically demanding, spread the work over several weekends.

raised-bed planting

right: **Growing plants in raised beds offers many benefits: The beds are easy to work, soil drains well, and walls double as seating. Fill beds with your own soil mix, rich in organic amendments, such as compost and rotted manure.**

1 **design** Plan the course of your wall using a rope or garden hose to define the bed shape. Mark the line on your lawn with spray paint or flour. To set the level of the wall, hammer stakes into the ground along the line. Mark the height of the wall on each stake. Connect the marks with a taut string. Use a level to make sure the height is even. Excavate turf and soil to a depth of 6 inches.

2 **stack** Add 2 inches of sand for a base. Choose the largest stones for the first layer; tilt them slightly down and back. Follow this tilting pattern for subsequent layers to increase wall stability. Fill the crevices between and behind stones with soil; stones should fit snugly together and not rock in place. Stagger the stones, leaving no uninterrupted vertical seams running from the top to the bottom of the wall.

3 **plant** Place each stone with the most attractive edge facing out. Use the taut string to guide your stacking efforts so you build to the correct height. If your site is sloping, adjust the string's height to compensate for the slope so that the finished wall appears level. Finish the top of the wall with large, flat stones. If you want plants to grow from the wall itself, leave spaces between stones to create planting pockets.

fences

fence finery

Choose a fence style that suits both your home
and garden, blending the two in an architecturally
cohesive way. The style of fencing you choose
depends largely on the purpose of the barrier.
For instance, a solid fence promises long-lasting
privacy; a row of vinyl pickets offers an
opportunity to build an easy-care, decorative
barrier. Craft pickets from fruit tree prunings or
another material that's handy and relevant to your
garden room's style. Posts and rails alone make
a simple, rustic divider.

Change the look of traditional fencing by using
bold-hue paint or stain. Use the same method to
turn a usually formal wrought-iron fence into an
electric-blue (or -red or -yellow) wonder.

Push the limits of boundary building by
combining wooden fences and masonry walls
to create hardworking structural elements in the
landscape. Concrete or stone constructions allow
you to include a pizza oven, grill, fireplace, or
fountain. Or intermingle architectural structures
with sections of living fence.

Top your fence with lattice strips to increase the
level of privacy and style. Add finishing touches to
posts. Top them with finials, from concrete acorns
or copper caps to wooden pyramids or spheres.

aspire higher

right: Disguised as a raised planter, a retaining
wall reaches new heights when its design
includes a fireplace, flue, and fencing. The
stucco fireplace makes the patio a favored
place. Latticework atop the fence adds visual
interest and avoids a stockade effect.

fence bends
left: Curved-rail fencing cuts an artful swath around established trees and flower beds. Use vinyl or recycled lumber to eliminate painting.

salvage style
below left: Reusing parts from two old fences and interspersing the two styles of pickets yields a fresh look. The stone-topped posts add personality.

wood wellness

You have options for finishing wooden garden structures to seal and protect them from weather. Finishes affect the look of the wood and its maintenance.

- **water repellant:** Including fungicide; protects structures from weather as wood turns gray over time; lasts up to 2 years.

- **paint:** Exterior grade in vast color choices; requires priming and reapplication every 3 to 5 years.

- **penetrating stain:** Mildew resistant; includes color and lasts up to 10 years between applications without priming.

- **transparent stain:** With ultraviolet inhibitor; enhances the wood's natural color up to 2 years.

creative corral

A fence defines garden room boundaries in a decorative way that's typically more open to airflow and less expensive than a wall. The height of the fence depends on your goal. Privacy dictates fences be at least head high, but traffic flow on adjacent sidewalks and intersections calls for structures between knee and waist high.

Combine design, construction materials, and paint or stain color to build a not-too-confining barrier that's a handsome landscape backdrop. Solid board panels, lattice, copper pipes, and window planting shelves give this fence (*right*) a distinctive style that lets light and air through while partially obstructing views of passersby.

The effectiveness of a fence depends on its positioning too. This one wraps around part of a front yard, screening the driveway and sidewalk. As climbing roses mature and drape the fence, it appears more and more to have sprouted in place.

Before you build, consider using fence-post anchors, which enable you to install fence posts temporarily or permanently without digging holes or pouring concrete. Instead, you drive a hollow spike into the ground and stand a post in it.

blended fence

right and *below:* The cedar fence suits the brick cottage and perennial gardens that it shields. Narrowly spaced copper pipes produce the look of shutters. Sheets of copper cover plant ledges, which offer a window to the world.

1 dig Lay out the site using stakes and strings; mark post placement with stakes. Use cedar or pressure-treated wood for bottom rails (2×4s) and posts (4×4s or 6×6s). Set posts 6 to 8 feet apart, depending on the size of the fence sections you build or buy. Use a (rented) posthole digger or an auger to make the holes 2 feet deep. Cover the bottom of the hole with 6 inches of gravel and insert the post. Check each post for plumb, using a level. Nail temporary braces to hold the posts in place.

2 fill Mix quick-set concrete according to the manufacturer's instructions. Shovel concrete into the hole around the post, taking care not to bump the post. Have a helper tamp the concrete, using a broom handle or wood scrap, to remove air bubbles. Round off the top of the concrete above the soil line; mounding the concrete allows water to drain away from the post. Let the concrete set at least 24 hours before hanging the lower fence rails; otherwise, you might force the posts out of alignment.

3 hang Attach the bottom fence rails to the posts. Choose a less expensive grade of rot-resistant lumber for the upper rails and fencing. Join rails to posts using galvanized rail clips. Purchase hot-dip galvanized hardware to reduce rust. Use a string and line level and a combination square to ensure that each rail is level and square with the posts. Paint or stain posts, rails, and fencing before nailing or screwing fencing in place.

fences: bamboo trellis

cost	make it	skill
$	1 day per panel	easy

you will need

ten or twelve 8-foot-long bamboo poles, about 2 inches in diameter

power drill, saw

galvanized or plastic-coated 1/16-inch wire

eight 2-inch deck screws or stainless-steel screws

table saw

wall decor

Walls produce instant privacy, a basic tenet for creating a garden room. View a wall as a blank canvas begging for color and add that color courtesy of garden art, collectible displays, or skyward-scampering vines. Our easy-to-build bamboo panels weave a touch of Asia into any room and do double duty as trellises.

Make quarter-rounds by cutting each bamboo pole in half lengthwise, then cutting each piece in half lengthwise again. Set aside four 8-foot-long bamboo quarters for frame rails. Cut two of the remaining bamboo quarters into two 3-foot-long pieces for vertical frame rails and one 2-foot-long piece for a shorter strip.

Build each frame by arranging two 3-foot and two 8-foot bamboo quarters in a rectangle, with ends overlapping. Place the remaining 3-foot and 8-foot bamboo quarters on top of this frame to form the front of the structure. Drill a 1/8-inch hole through the ends of each piece where they intersect at the corners. Wire the pieces together at the four corners. Adjust the rectangle until it's straight.

fence finery

right: **Dress up a plain wooden fence with latticework panels. This project makes wall trellises from bamboo but could just as easily use prefabricated latticework for the construction.**

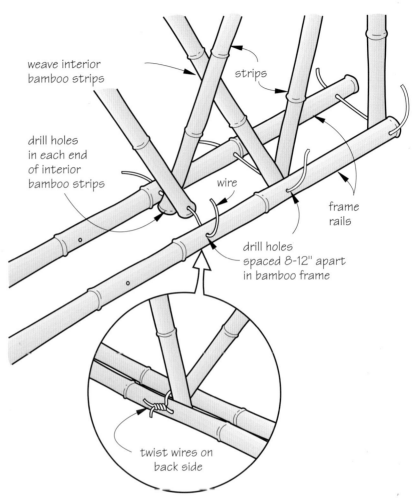

weave interior
bamboo strips

strips

drill holes
in each end
of interior
bamboo strips

wire

frame
rails

drill holes
spaced 8-12" apart
in bamboo frame

twist wires on
back side

Cut the remaining 8-foot bamboo quarters into
4-foot strips. Insert several diagonally and parallel
to one another, about 6 inches apart, between the
front and rear frames. Roughly size, cut, and add
shorter diagonal strips near the frame corners
to fill out the lattice design. Insert the remaining
diagonal pieces in the opposite direction, using an
over-under basket-weaving technique. The ends of
opposing diagonals should intersect one another at
the frames. Drill ⅛-inch holes at these intersecting
points, and wire the layers of bamboo together.
Use screws to mount your panel to a fence or wall.

fences: custom pickets

cost	make it	skill
$$	2 weekends	moderate

you will need

- two 6×6-inch posts (56 inches long plus depth of frost line) (A)
- two 2×8×7½-inch post caps (B)
- two decorative finials (C)
- two 2×4s (8 feet long) for end boards (D)
- two 2×3s (8 feet long) for rails (E)
- five 1×4s (8 feet long) for spacers (F)
- four 1×8s (10 feet long) for pickets (G)
- scrap of ¼-inch plywood (for quail template)
- router
- exterior-grade weatherproof adhesive
- zinc-plated screws and galvanized nails
- concrete premix
- jigsaw or scroll saw
- circular, table, or radial-arm saw
- drill
- hammer
- screwdriver
- exterior-grade polyurethane or stain
- posthole digger

picket pizzazz
right: Merge fun and function by building a fence with shapely pickets. Develop your own picket design, using the quail dimensions *(opposite)* as a guide.

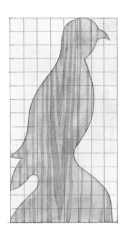

1 square = 1 inch

quail-topped fence

Pairs of quails keep watch over house and garden in this imaginative take on traditional pickets. Start with rot–resistant wood, which stands up to the elements (cedar, redwood, or pressure-treated lumber). Posts should be rated for ground contact. The materials list (*opposite*) makes one fence section 8 feet, 9½ inches long, including posts. Preassemble each fence section in your work area; then take sections outdoors and attach them to the posts.

make the posts Chamfer the four edges of each post (A) with a router (see diagram at *left*). For each cap (B), rout a 7½×7½×1½-inch square stock with a cove bit. Use exterior-grade weatherproof adhesive and galvanized nails to attach caps to posts. Drill a pilot hole in the center of each cap and screw in a finial (C).

build the parts Round off ends and edges of two 2×4-inch end boards (D). Cut two 2×3-inch rails (E) 91½ inches long. Drill pilot holes and drive zinc-plated screws through the end boards into the rail end to fasten them securely. Make sure the rails are square with the end boards.

Cut eight 60-inch-long pickets (G). Enlarge the quail pattern (*above left*), transfer it to plywood, and cut a template for shaping pickets. Cut quails in pickets using a scroll saw or jigsaw.

Cut 1×4s to length and round the ends to form the five spacers (F). Nail pickets and spacers to rails, spacing them 1 inch apart. Help preserve the wood by treating it with an exterior-grade clear polyurethane or stain. Follow product directions for application.

fasten the fence Set and plumb posts (for more about this, see page 85). Drive screws through the end boards (D) into the posts to install the preassembled fence section.

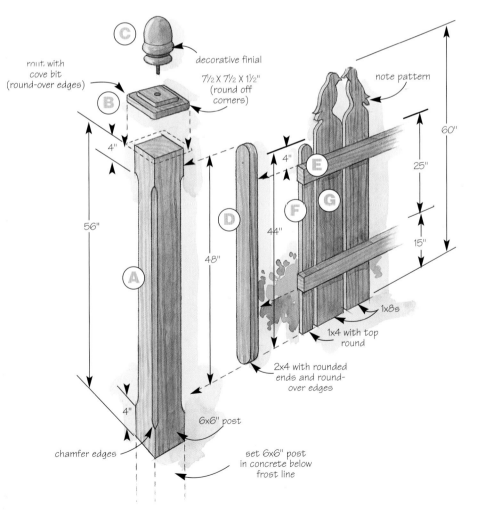

rout with cove bit (round-over edges)

decorative finial

7½ X 7½ X 1½" (round off corners)

note pattern

4"

4"

60"

25"

56"

15"

48"

44"

1x8s

1x4 with top round

2x4 with rounded ends and round-over edges

4"

6x6" post

chamfer edges

set 6x6" post in concrete below frost line

yard & garden projects | **89**

fences: living fence

cost	make it	skill
$$	3 growing seasons	easy

you will need

- three or more dwarf fruit trees
- posthole digger (optional)
- 4×4 posts
- 2×4 top rail (8 feet long)
- 14-gauge wire
- hand pruners
- cloth-covered wire plant ties

especially espalier

Train dwarf fruit trees using standard pruning techniques to form a living wall and enjoy the privacy and fresh produce it yields. In an espalier (pronounced es-PAL-yay), plants grow along a usually flat, symmetrical framework against a wall, trellis, or freestanding form. Frequent pruning and tying of new growth directs plants into a rigid pattern, such as intersecting diamonds (right) or horizontal arms or elbows.

Plan your espalier and research patterns to fit your needs. The traditional Belgian fence (shown right) forms an airy, artistic barrier. Use espalier to convert narrow planting beds along driveways or walls into productive gardens. For espalier fruit fences, choose dwarf varieties of apples, peaches, or pears. Train a purely ornamental fence by choosing a blooming tree or shrub, such as flowering crabapple, magnolia, or double-file viburnum.

edible walls

right and *far right:* Select fruit tree varieties that boast disease resistance, such as 'Jonafree' apples, to create a more carefree fence. Other good apple choices include 'MacFree' and 'Freedom'.

1 support Select an overall pattern for your espalier. Build an appropriate framework of stout posts (8 feet apart), a top rail, and heavy-gauge wire horizontal supports. Stretch wire tautly from post to post, spaced vertically at 1-foot intervals, to create a framework. If you train trees against a wall, leave 12 inches between the structure and the support system to allow for maintenance and air circulation. Plant 2- or 3-year-old dwarf trees at least an arm's length apart.

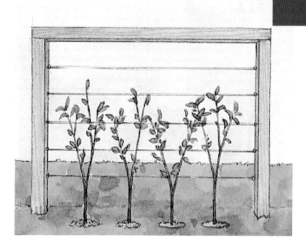

2 anchor Make planting holes at least twice the diameter of the plant's root ball. Plant trees slightly in front of the wire supports. Refill the planting holes and water thoroughly. Water young trees weekly during their first summer and fall if rain is lacking. Cut off branches extending to the back or front; leave branches reaching to the sides. If you train trees along a wall, position a nail or an eye hook in the wall near intersecting branches. Loosely twist a plant tie around the branches and the hook.

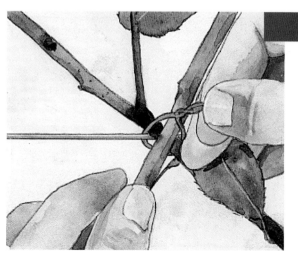

3 train Crisscross branches from neighboring trees to train them into the desired pattern. Twist a plant tie around the branches and the wire to secure them, leaving room for branch growth. Over the next three or so years, prune and train trees in late winter. As the trees grow, continue to cross and tie the branches to the framework, snipping unwanted growth to maintain the pattern. Remove fruit buds the first two years to concentrate the tree's energy into growing branches. Look for fruit in the third year.

fences: lattice

classic camouflage

When it comes to garden cover-ups, lattice reigns as a popular and classic choice. Standing solo or swathed in vines, a section of latticework effectively hides, surrounds, or otherwise encloses elements in the garden. Whether concealing air-conditioning units or garbage cans, lattice lavishes stylistic charm over the unsightly necessities of life. Tacked onto the sides of a prefabricated garden shed, latticework dresses up dullness while providing the perfect place to hang tools.

Whatever your garden's style, lattice blends form and function. Choose from prefabricated, 4×8-foot panels available in a variety of patterns at lumberyards or home centers. Or turn your creativity loose to construct homemade panels of lath or bamboo. Either way, use the lacy network of woven strips to make decorative screens that limit the view without blocking it.

When shaping garden rooms, use lattice to form boundaries that let in breezes and sunshine. This may be a big plus in a small area with limited exposure. Use latticework screens to surround a dining nook or encircle a spa. Hide utility meters behind an appropriate-size framed panel.

The peekaboo structure of lattice enhances mystery in the garden, especially when draped in vines. Let annual flowering vines smother a lattice panel, or establish perennial climbers, such as hops, clematis, trumpet vine, or climbing hydrangea, to soften the sections with concealing foliage.

screened scene

right: Vinyl lattice panels, topped with a curved rail and detailed pergola, conceal a family's backyard living room. A tangle of morning glory vines flourishes on the structure.

1 garden weave

Garden-style lattice features 3-inch openings. This pattern will provide privacy after the vines scramble up and over the panels. Use this lattice as a support or windbreak for plants or for added privacy.

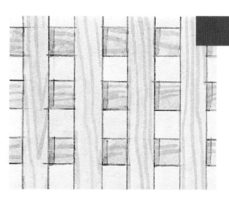

2 vertical and horizontal

Choose a lattice pattern and size based on your intended use. For a carport, 6-inch-wide openings let plenty of light and air through. Conceal garbage cans or a compost pile using lattice with a smaller opening size, such as 1½ inches.

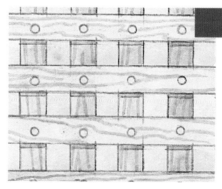

3 circles and squares

Latticework styles and their decorative effects vary. Customize a standard grid by drilling holes at the points where strips intersect. Use this lattice in areas that require airflow, such as in narrow passageways or damp courtyards.

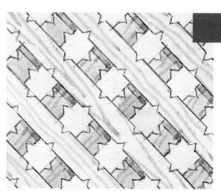

4 notched Star-shape illusions results when notched lattice strips come together to create a panel with a designer touch. Purchase prefabricated panels crafted with notched strips, or customize them by shaping strips and cobbling your own stylized motif.

yard & garden projects | **93**

fences: gates

through the garden gate

An effective garden gate demands forethought. The
right blend of materials and design welcomes guests
without surrendering your sense of security. Aim
to blend or contrast the gate with the site. For
high-traffic, main-entrance gates, consider durability
as well as decorative details. Wrought iron promises
low maintenance and long wear; wooden entries
require restaining or repainting over time. For
a natural look, bamboo boasts remarkable wear
without upkeep; a rustic branch-and-twig structure
offers charm at little cost but won't last a lifetime.

Top a gate with an arch to create a grand
entrance. Install a self-locking latch and make
a handy exit for the kids. Hang gates with
weatherproof hardware, and anchor them
to sturdy posts for strength and endurance.

ornate gate
above right: **An
8-foot-tall wrought-
iron gate teams with
an accompanying
fence to present
sophisticated
security. Greenery
blends the structures
with the site and
enhances privacy.**

home sweet home
right: **A waist-level
gate in a picket fence
suits a cottage-style
house and garden
and announces the
point of entry. Paired
with a clematis-
covered arch, it's
perfectly inviting.**

stylish entrée

left: Embellish the entry to your home and garden with a gable-top cedar gate. The double swinging doors allow a generous, 6-foot-wide entry—ample room to fit a couple of people or a garden cart through it. The gate design complements the fence motif. The roof affords shelter on inclement days and is an easy-to-add element for an existing gate. Install lighting near your gate, and include climbing plants to complete the scene.

ceilings

over the top

What's the surest way to transform an area of the garden into a room? Cap it with a ceiling. Coverings for garden retreats range from the strictly architectural to a soft canopy of fabric or foliage.

Think about how you intend to use the room before determining the ceiling's style, allowing for sunbeams and starlight or for keeping out the weather. If you plan to fill the room with cozy-cushioned furniture, you'll want more substantial coverage than if you outfit the space with a weather-worthy teak or shorea furniture ensemble. A simple pergola provides an easy-to-build covering for a room. Plant vines at the base of the posts to form a living ceiling.

garden getaway

above: Gently arched beams and 2×2s form a slatted roof that tempers the midday sun and allows glimpses of sky and trees. Posts and railings edge an 8-foot-square wooden deck. Architectural details, such as the capitals and keystone, echo trim on the house.

blooming abandon

left: A simple pergola, crowned with a tangle of soft pink bougainvillea, encloses a garden room that's rich with personality. Teak benches invite lingering, and a flagstone floor keeps feet dry on dewy mornings. Roses fill the room with scent.

ceilings: awning

colorful canopy

Now you see it; now you don't. That's the story of a retractable awning. Fully extended, it casts cooling shade; rolled up, it permits sunshine to splash freely onto the patio and into interior rooms.

A retractable awning helps control light levels on a sun-exposed side of a house and saves energy costs. It also protects interior furnishings from sun-induced fading. Equipped with a motorized, tubular frame and internal wiring that runs into the house, the awning moves at the touch of a switch, extending to its full or partial potential.

Select awning fabrics that complement your home's architectural style and facade. If you want the awning to serve as a flashy focal point, lean toward bright tones. For a canopy that blends beautifully into the surroundings, choose hues that echo exterior shades found in the house color, trim, or shingles. Select fabric patterns proportionate to the size of your house and the awning. Small stripes look busy on a large expanse of fabric; wide-stripe patterns overwhelm small homes. Stylish touches, such as contrasting trim, scalloped or keyhole valances, or tassels, perk up a solid-tone awning. Peruse your awning contractor's portfolio to view style and fabric options that look good on homes similar to yours.

roof on the move
above right: **Retract a motorized awning when you want to increase the light indoors or during high winds. This retracted awning fits snugly against the house.**

made in the shade
right: **Measuring 10×25 feet, this awning fits neatly over the recessed front entryway and creates a welcoming, shaded room.**

courtyard style

left: The heavy-duty fabric awning extends over a cozy seating area. When the retractable canopy was installed, a flagstone-and-gravel floor was added along with a table, chairs, and fragrant perennials to create an outdoor living room. The striped awning coordinates with the trim color of the house. As with most custom-made awnings, the tubular steel framework, weatherproof fabric, and operating mechanism were installed by the manufacturer.

ceilings: vine canopy

sheltering leaves

Train vines to weave a living ceiling anywhere in your garden that you desire shelter: between the house and the garage, over a patio or a deck, or in any area that could benefit from added shade. To begin, build a framework for the vines to climb and cover. Set posts (or brackets) into place for uprights; connect them with side rails. Run multistrand steel wires between the rails, forming a scaffold. Determine a pattern for the canopy based on the degree of coverage you want. For a long-lived ceiling, use perennial vines: climbing hydrangea, trumpet vine, ivy, wisteria, or clematis. In warmer climates, plant bougainvillea, jasmine, sky vine, or cat-claw creeper. Choose vines appropriate to your region's climate and the site's sun exposure.

leafy ceiling

left: A driveway between two historic Boston buildings needed shade. The owner wanted to spruce up the overhead space between the apartment buildings while preserving their architecture. To create a living roof, she planted three wisteria vines. The vines scrambled up to iron brackets along the sunny side of one of the buildings and twined their way across multistrand steel wires. It took four years for wisteria growth to cover the grid. Annual trimming requires a stepladder, a sharp pair of hand pruners, and a good sense of balance.

romance in bloom

left: The delightfully fragrant and colorful blooms of wisteria dangle from vines like clusters of grapes. The secret to a rich crop of flowers is properly timed pruning. Late-summer or early-fall pruning in cold climates gives vines ample time to set flower buds for the following spring. Prune during winter in warm climates.

gimme shelter

Arbors, trellises, fences, and other structures provide a framework for a garden, giving it form and enhancing its function. Structures help direct views and traffic through the garden. In addition to providing shelter, structural components define garden areas, create a sense of enclosure, and establish the boundaries between your property and your neighbors.

stylish embellishments Above all, garden structures illustrate a garden's style, with their architectural form and material aesthetics. A pergola or a gazebo design should echo or complement the style of your house.

Ideally, the construction materials will also help blend the house and the garden. A traditional garden arch suits almost any house and garden, whether a simple structure of painted wood, sturdy metal, bent branches, or lattice. Combined with adjoining fencing and planted with vines or roses, the structure becomes a magnificent focal point.

what goes where Deliberately place a stylish arbor where it establishes a welcoming entry to the garden or an attractive transition from one area to another. Site a gazebo, a pergola, a tepee, or other shelter wherever you want an instant outdoor room.

Coordinate garden structures with new or existing plantings and your efforts will transform a yard into a destination. Climbing roses and flowering perennial vines usually become well established and begin to sprawl over a structure by their third year, so have patience with plants and gently guide them to fit a structure.

arbors

theme variations

Use arbors to frame a
view, to greet guests,
to provide a place for
sitting, or to give the
garden a sculptural feel.
Arbors not only draw
you along a garden
path, they provide
a place for vines to
scramble skyward.

Most often, people
associate an arbor with
an entrance, indicating
a passage from one
area of the garden to
another. Enhance this
sensation with a little
architectural sleight
of hand. Intensify the
demarcating effect of
an arbor by expanding
its borders. Add to the
arbor's structure with

artful arch

right: A blend of
cedar and wrought
iron forms an arbor
that's long-lasting
and weather
resistant. Use
metal to incorporate
curves into traditional
right-angle designs.

raised planters, built-in benches, or lattice-topped extensions (shown *opposite*).

Position surfaces underfoot to reflect the transition from one garden area to another. A simple, affordable treatment entails laying brick or flagstone directly beneath an arbor and slowly fading it into gravel or mulch pathways on either side of the arbor. Decorate your arbor with annual or perennial vines that offer color and shade. For freestanding arbors, surround the structure with an abundance of lush shrubs, such as hydrangeas, shrub roses, and Korean lilacs, to form living walls and create a sense of privacy.

gaining strength
above left: Gussy up a gate to do more than usher guests into the garden. Adding substantive concrete pillars, a top dressing of rail rafters, and a clematis vine creates garden sculpture.

rooftop creativity
left: With the posts of an arbor in place, turn your imagination loose and choose the covering overhead. This scrap-metal mesh lets the sun shine on the brick patio below.

105

arbors: traditional entry

cost	make it	skill
$$	2 days	moderate

you will need

- shovel
- two 4×4 posts (11 feet long)
- gravel
- concrete
- two 2×6s (6 feet long) (crossbeams)
- stepladder
- framing square
- eight galvanized lag screws
- ratchet
- jigsaw
- two 2×6s (7 feet long)
- hammer
- galvanized nails
- twenty–six 2×2 rails (45 inches long)
- exterior–grade stain or paint

stylish arbors

Of all the useful garden structures, arbors offer modest scale and endless style variations. Arching or standing straight and squared, they fulfill many functions in the garden, from creating a private hideaway to defining a path. Joined with fencing, an arbor shapes a classic garden entry. When coupled with a swing or bench, an arbor beckons for solitary reflection or intimate moments.

Consider views through the arbor in both directions when choosing its location. In a large garden, install an arbor partway down a path to invite visitors to explore what lies beyond. In a small garden, use an arbor to create an impression that the garden extends beyond it.

Choose a style that blends into the surrounding plantings and rooms. For durability, select an arbor crafted from pressure-treated wood, metal, or plastic. Use the materials list and instructions to make an arbor similar to the one pictured.

grand entrance

right: **If the arbor is near your house, select a construction material and design that complement your home's architecture.**

1 posts Dig holes for posts (see page 85). Space the posts no more than 6 feet apart. (If you want to extend the distance, increase the beam size to 2×8.) Pour 6 inches of gravel in the holes, insert posts, and fill with concrete. Cut two 6-foot-long 2×6s into four 3-foot-long crossbeams. They will define the depth of the arbor. Standing on a stepladder, use lag screws to secure the 2×6s to both sides of each post. Use a framing square to align the crossbeams with the posts before tightening the screws.

2 beams Shape the decorative detail at the ends of the 7-foot-long 2×6 beams using a jigsaw. Design an end treatment to match your home's architecture or other structures in the garden. Attach the beams to the crossbeams by driving at least two galvanized nails through the 2×6s into the ends of the crossbeams. You'll need help with this step. Have your partner hold the loose end of each 2×6 until you nail it into position. Cut and install optional arching crosspieces.

3 rails Cut 2×2 rails to length. Position the first one carefully, then drive one nail through each end of the rail into the 2×6 beams beneath. Lay an extra piece of 2×2 against the first rail to determine spacing for the next and subsequent rails; ensure that each rail extends equally over the beams before nailing. Stain or paint the arbor either before or after constructing it. Plant vines, such as climbing roses, honeysuckle, or jasmine, to create a passageway that's filled with fragrance.

arbors: elegant entry

cost	make it	skill
$$	weekend	moderate

you will need

four 2×4s
(10 feet long) (A)

four 1×4s
(8 feet long) (B)

thirteen 2×2s (4 feet
long), or seven 2×2s
(8 feet long) cut in
half, or 13 precut
deck spindles (C)

72 feet of lath, or
twenty–four 36–inch
pieces (D and E)

exterior–grade
construction adhesive

approximately sixty
3–inch deck screws

approximately thirty
2–inch deck screws

approximately twelve
1⅞–inch deck
screws (for brackets;
optional)

approximately fifty
6d galvanized nails

3–4 gallons gravel

exterior–grade latex
stain or polyurethane
sealer (optional)

quick coverage

right: Choose arbor-
enhancing vines, such
as annual morning
glory, cypress vine,
or thunbergia, for
easy color from
seed that lingers
until frost. Compost
vines after frost.

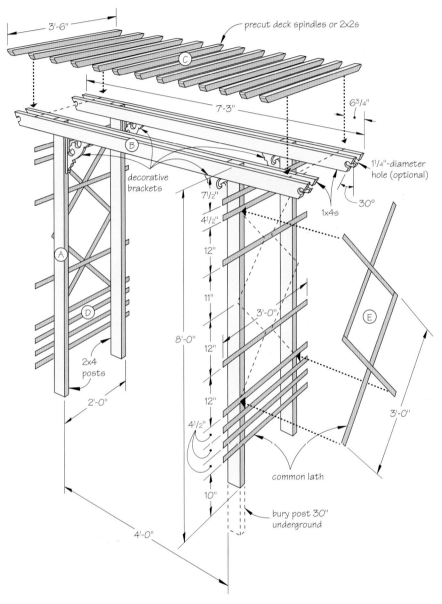

precut deck spindles or 2x2s

3'-6"

C

7'-3"

6³/₄"

B

1¼"-diameter
hole (optional)

decorative
brackets

7½"

4½"

1x4s

30°

12"

A

11"

D

3'-0"

E

8'-0"

12"

2x4
posts

3'-0"

2'-0"

12"

4½"

common lath

10"

bury post 30"
underground

4'-0"

welcome, friends!

The price tags of many arbors (even those made from kits) soar as high as the structures themselves. This entry arbor is affordable, elegant, and easy to build.

Begin with rot-resistant wood, such as cedar, redwood, or pressure-treated pine. Dig 30-inch-deep holes for the four main 2x4 posts (A). Add 6 inches of gravel to the holes for drainage.

Cut the four 1x4 top rails (B) into 7-foot, 3-inch lengths. To add the optional 1¼-inch decorative hole, mark the hole and 30-degree ends before cutting rails. Drill the hole with a 1¼-inch flat bit; then cut off the end along the marked line.

If you didn't purchase precut deck spindles, cut the thirteen 2x2s (C) to 3-foot, 6-inch pieces, adding a 45-degree bevel on both ends. Cut the common lath (D) into twenty-four 3-foot pieces.

sides Lay the four uprights (A) side by side on their narrow sides on a flat surface with the ends flush. Measure and mark lattice locations (D and E) on all four sides. To make each end section, lay two post pieces on the ground 2 feet apart. Nail horizontal lath pieces (D), attaching bottom and top ones first. After all the horizontals are mounted, attach the diagonals (E). Set the two assembled sections into the postholes; plumb with braces. Fill the holes with a mixture of soil and gravel.

top Lay the four top rails (B) narrow side up; measure and mark the spacing (4½ inches apart) for the 13 top pieces (C). Attach the top rails with 2-inch deck screws; use 3-inch deck screws to fasten the top pieces in place. Apply construction adhesive at all joints to increase stability. If you're using decorative brackets, attach them using 1⅝-inch deck screws. Apply a coat of exterior-grade latex stain or polyurethane sealer, if desired, to help protect the wood against weather.

pergolas

made in the shade

When your yard contains little more than hot, dry space, create an inviting oasis of cooling shade and uncover many options for outdoor living. A simple pergola provides cover overhead; vines form a verdant canopy. Design a pergola with graceful columns to add structure and visual impact in your landscape. Create a look similar to this scene *(right)* by hiring a concrete contractor to pour concrete columns in large cardboard tubes. When the tubes are cut away, they leave a circular swirl in the concrete. Choose to blend the lines, or leave them in place; use a sandblaster to give texture and an aged-looking finish to the columns.

Ask the concrete professional to set eye hooks in the tops of the columns for anchoring the pergola's steel-wire framework. Using heavy-duty wire,

form a taut framework from column to column. Weave wires into an overall grid.

Train perennial vines to climb the columns and grow over the grid. Plant wisteria, climbing roses, clematis, trumpet vine, ivy, climbing hydrangea, or akebia. Trim vines to keep them neat looking.

fired up

left: **An elegant outdoor room replaces a plain backyard with a concrete terrace, a fireplace, and a mosaic-embellished chimney. Concrete columns support a wisteria-draped pergola. The room proves inviting and cool in hot weather, cozy and comfortable when the weather turns chilly. An added grill rack can turn the fireplace into a cooker.**

pergolas: basic

cost	make it	skill
$$	3 days	moderate

you will need

- four 6×6 posts (10 feet long)
- compound miter saw
- drill
- eight 2×8 crossbeams (18 feet long)
- four 2×10 main beams (16 feet long)
- builder's square
- sixteen 9-inch carriage bolts
- eleven 2×4 rafters
- wood screws, lag screws
- shovel

hillside hideaway

Cope with a sloping site by perching a pergola atop it. The hillside landing supplies a level surface for a pergola furnished with a patio and roomy chairs.

Retaining walls buttress the stairs and provide a place to heap soil from the bank to form raised flower beds. Stairs master the steep grade with ease, occupying little space, and traversing the incline in a way that won't make it an arduous climb.

Plant a hillside with ground-hugging plants to control erosion and eliminate mowing. Traditional groundcovers, such as bugleweed, pachysandra, periwinkle, or hosta, quickly cover a bank with greenery. Vines also carpet slopes with color. Try ivy, clematis, honeysuckle, or Virginia creeper. Scotch broom, groundcover rose ('Flower Carpet'), Japanese juniper (*Juniperus procumbens*), and cotoneaster are shrubs that can handle hills. Plant densely to fill in the area within the first two growing seasons.

pergola retreat

right: Tackle an incline by topping it with a pergola. Roses and wisteria surround the room with seasonal appeal.

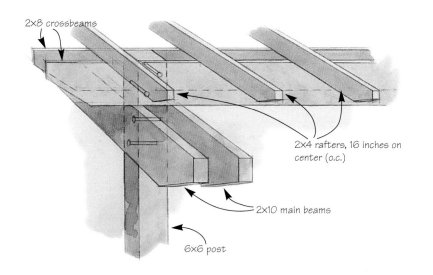

2×8 crossbeams

2×4 rafters, 16 inches on center (o.c.)

2×10 main beams

6×6 post

build a basic pergola

No matter where you place a pergola (on a terraced slope, over a patio, or extending from the house), this 12×14-foot structure (*below left*) is a project that those with modest carpentry skills can tackle. Follow these plans and instructions to build a comparable pergola or customize them to suit your needs.

Set posts as described on page 85. Measure down $7\frac{1}{4}$ inches from the top of each post and mark a line indicating the top edge of each main beam. Then, with the aid of a friend, attach the four main beams (in pairs) to the posts, with one beam running along each side of the post. Insert carriage bolts through predrilled holes. Add the four pairs of crossbeams (2×8s). Bolt the two outside pairs of crossbeams to the posts in the same way you attached the main beams. Use wood screws, angled through the crossbeams into the main beams, to hold the inner two pairs of beams in place. Finally, install the 11 rafters (2×4s) on top of the crossbeams, using 5-inch lag screws.

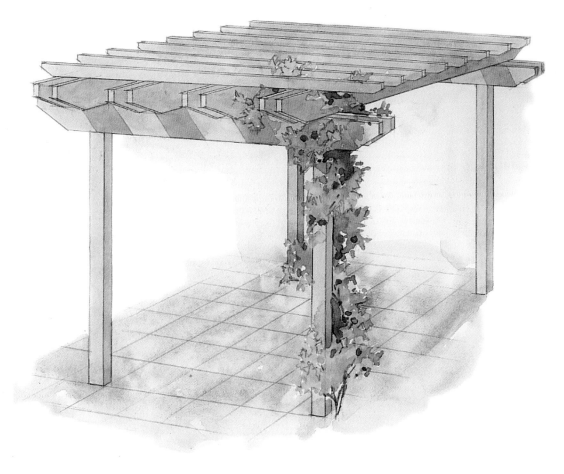

pergolas: bamboo

cost	make it	skill
$$$	4 days	advanced

backyard resort

Cultivate the look, feel, and appeal of a resort with a garden room that's decked out with serene ambience and comfort. The space devoted to a get-away-from-it-all setting doesn't have to be large. This 10×14-foot deck boasts big style without taking up the entire backyard.

In small rooms, rely on built-in furnishings to make the most of space. Keep railings low and open to define the space without enclosing it. Designate areas for socializing or relaxing by arranging furniture appropriately. Leave an open area for children to play.

Building a breezy retreat as shown (right) requires carpentry skills. Tackle the project in stages, starting with the deck, adding the pergola, then completing deck railings, benches, and tabletops. Enlist professionals

sunscreen on high

right: A pergola covered in bamboo-and-reed matting screens the sun and withstands weather well. Bamboo lasts long, especially in climates with freeze-thaw cycles. A thatched roof made with reed lasts for decades.

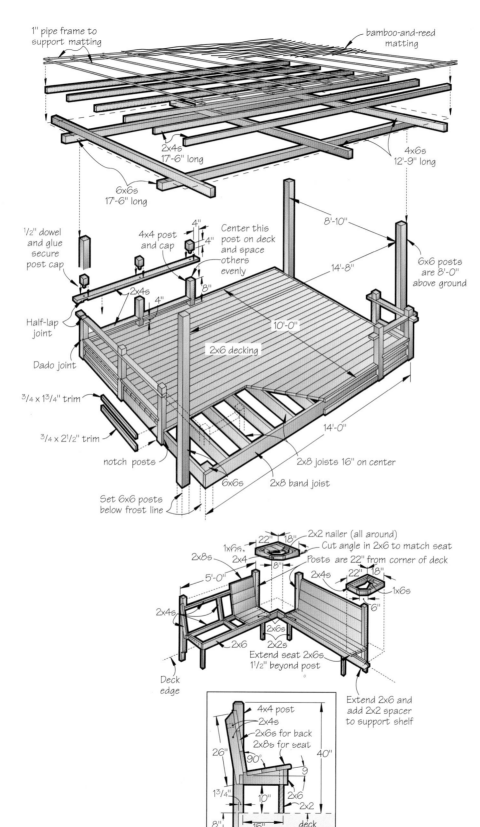

1" pipe frame to support matting

bamboo-and-reed matting

2x4s 17'-6" long

4x6s 12'-9" long

6x6s 17'-6" long

1/2" dowel and glue secure post cap

4x4 post and cap

4"

4"

Center this post on deck and space others evenly

8'-10"

6x6 posts are 8'-0" above ground

2x4s

4"

8"

14'-8"

Half-lap joint

Dado joint

10'-0"

2x6 decking

3/4 x 1 3/4" trim

3/4 x 2 1/2" trim

notch posts

Set 6x6 posts below frost line

6x6s

2x8 band joist

2x8 joists 16" on center

14'-0"

2x2 nailer (all around)
Cut angle in 2x6 to match seat
Posts are 22" from corner of deck

22" 18"

1x6s

2x8s

2x4

8"

5'-0"

2x4s

22" 18"

1x6s

2x4s

6"

2x4s

2x6

2x6s

2x2s

Extend seat 2x6s 1 1/2" beyond post

Deck edge

Extend 2x6 and add 2x2 spacer to support shelf

4x4 post
2x4s
2x6s for back
2x8s for seat

26"

90°

40"

9

1 3/4"

10"

2x6

2x2

8"

15"

deck

to do all or part of the work if you prefer.

To begin, set posts in the ground below the frost line in your region. See page 85 for details. Build the deck, mounting the perimeter 2x8 band joists in place first, then adding the 2x8 joists. Use wood screws to hold decking in place. Screw the roof beams (6x6s and 4x6s) and crossbars (2x4s) in place. Use wire to assemble the pipe frame for the roof; attach it to the crossbars with nails driven through predrilled holes. Wire the bamboo-and-reed matting to the pipe frame. Build rails along the deck edges. Construct the benches and tabletops; attach them to the decking.

Purchase thatching or bamboo-and-reed matting from Internet or mail-order suppliers or from garden centers. Evaluate samples in terms of shade-casting ability and weatherability before selecting a roofing material.

pergolas: arch

cost	make it	skill
$$$	3 days	moderate

you will need

- shovel
- gravel or crushed rock
- four 6×6 posts
- quick-set concrete
- nineteen 2×6s (12 feet long)
- eight 2×12s (8 feet long)
- four 1×12s (10 feet long)
- wood screws
- wood putty
- wood sealer (optional)
- exterior-grade primer and paint or stain (optional)

arched elegance

The open nature of a pergola lends a sense of luxurious spaciousness to a garden area that can't afford to be a fully enclosed room. Those space-constrained instances include rooms in front yards, narrow side yards, and tiny backyards. A pergola forms a room with clearly defined boundaries and unobstructed views. Most pergolas feature a roof of lattice weave or a grid of some sort. Celebrate outdoor living in grand style by constructing an arched roof that commands attention as an architectural feature and reflects the curving edges of nearby flower beds.

Inside the pergola, select flooring material that's durable and furniture-friendly. A bench or a pair of armchairs and a coffee table fit comfortably into this pergola. Choose weather-worthy fabrics when adding cushions. Mark the entrance to your pergola in formal style with a pair of globe-shape boxwood shrubs or matching topiaries.

private parlor

right: Create a place for conversation or contemplation by tucking a bench beneath a round-top pergola. A brick-and-stone floor completes the scene.

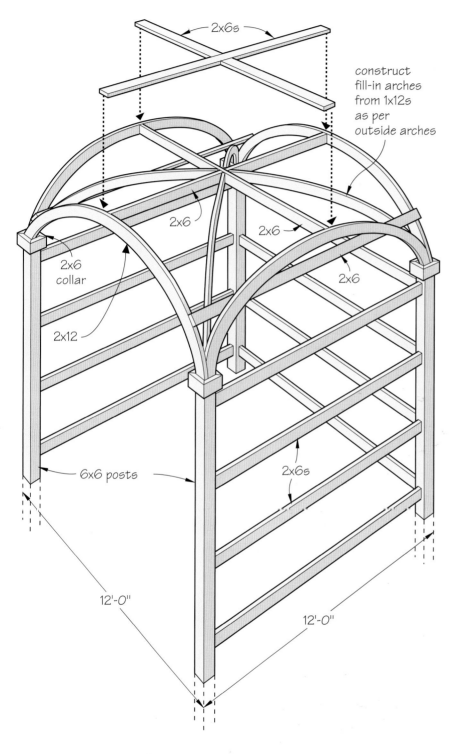

2x6s

construct
fill-in arches
from 1x12s
as per
outside arches

2x6

2x6

2x6
collar

2x6

2x12

6x6 posts

2x6s

12'-0"

12'-0"

build the arched pergola

Use the diagrams to construct a stylish pergola for your garden room. Adjust the dimensions and the materials to suit your space. Start with pressure-treated lumber or cedar for superior weatherability.

Set posts below the frost line. See page 85 for details. Trim ends from 2x6 crossbars to fit between posts; attach crossbars to posts using angled screws. Top posts with 2x6 collars. Construct the four outside arches from 2x12s using half-lap joints. Enlisting the help of a friend, position the arches atop the 2x6 post collars. Attach the 2x6 pieces to the arches as shown to stabilize them. Add the four fill-in arches. For a neat look, countersink all wood screws; then cover with wood putty. Apply a wood sealer to protect your structure and preserve the lumber's natural color; otherwise, let it weather. If you plan to stain or prime and paint your pergola, do so after construction.

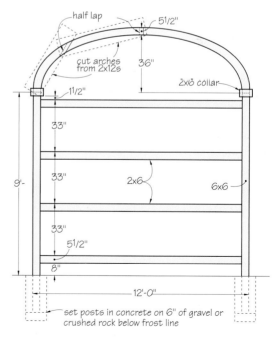

half lap

51/2"

cut arches
from 2x12s

36"

2x6 collar

11/2"

33"

33"

2x6

6x6

9'-

33"

51/2"

8"

12'-0"

set posts in concrete on 6" of gravel or
crushed rock below frost line

pergolas: swing

cost	make it	skill
$$$	2 weekends	moderate

you will need

two 4×6 posts (12 feet long), one 4×6 (8 feet long) for crosspiece

three 4×4 beams (10 feet long), one 4×4 (8 feet long) for braces

eight 2×2s (8 feet long) for top rails

compound miter saw

drill

lag screws: (four $^3/_8$×10 inches, twelve $^3/_8$×8 inches, four $^3/_8$×7 inches, four $^3/_8$×5 inches)

twenty-four flat washers ($^3/_8$ inch)

ratchet set

ninety deck screws, (3½ inches)

level

four bags premix concrete

two eyebolts ($^3/_8$×4 inches)

60-inch prefabricated swing

thirty feet of ½-inch rope

care-free seating

Garden swings are all about relaxing, kicking off your clogs, and letting the breeze tickle your toes. Combine a pergola or an arbor and a swing to create an eye-catching focal point that also provides luxurious seating.

A swing requires more than firm footing. It needs sturdy supports set deep into the ground. The structure (*right* and *opposite*) features 4×6 upright posts set in holes dug below the frost line. Both posts are held firmly in place with concrete premix (requiring only the addition of water). Dig your holes larger than the width of the posts so enough concrete can be poured in to provide support. Choose rot-resistant wood, such as cedar, redwood, or pressure-treated pine.

swingin' decor

right: Backed with a privacy fence and surrounded by fragrant plantings, this swing provides a pleasant retreat.

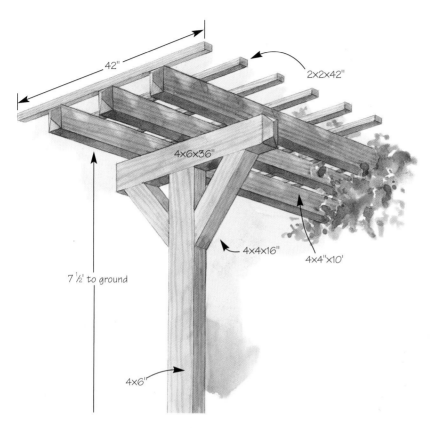

42"

2×2×42"

4×6×36"

4×4×16"

4×4"×10'

7 ½' to ground

4×6"

rope trick

left: **You don't have to be a magician to hang your swing with a cleverly placed rope. This supporting strand is laced through the swing's end upright via a ½-inch hole drilled through the wood. Rope works well to suspend a swing in climates without harsh freezes.**

pergola construction

Start with the materials list, *opposite.* Make the following cuts: For the crosspieces at each end, cut two 3-foot lengths from the 8-foot 4×6; for the angled braces at each end, cut four 16-inch pieces from the 8-foot 4×4; and for the top rails, cut 15 pieces, each 42 inches long, from the 8-foot 2×2s. Then cut 45-degree angles at each end of the four 16-inch pieces to complete the braces. (As a decorative option, angle-cut the ends of the 3-footers and the 10-foot-long roof beams.)

On a flat surface, preassemble the two vertical T-sections. For each T, first attach one of the 3-foot 4×6s perpendicular to the top of one of the 4×6 posts, using two $\frac{3}{8}$-inch-diameter, 10-inch-long lag screws. Then attach the angled braces, using one 5-inch and one 7-inch lag screw at each end of each brace. Use washers on all lag screws.

Then set and plumb each T-section in its hole (80 inches, center to center) and hold them in position with two temporary braces screwed to stakes in the ground. (Make sure both supports are the same height by laying one of the 10-foot 4×4s across the tops and checking for level.) Pour the concrete premix in the postholes and let it set for 24 hours.

Finish the job by attaching the three 4×4 beams to the tops of the two end supports with two $\frac{3}{8}$-inch-diameter, 8-inch-long lag screws, with a washer on each, at each junction. Then, starting about 3¼ inches from one end of the 4×4s, use 3½-inch deck screws (two at each junction) to attach the fifteen 2×2s crosswise, leaving 6½ inches between each 2×2.

Hang the swing from two $\frac{3}{8}$-inch-diameter eyebolts running vertically through the middle 4×4 beam. Suspend the swing with ropes or chains. If using rope, consult a guide to knot tying and find the three-strand eye splice; this nonslip hitch holds most swings securely.

gazebos

the view from here

The word *gazebo* comes from blending the words *gaze* and *about*. In the garden, a gazebo is not only a strong focal point, it also commands a vantage point. Position your gazebo to survey delightful scenery, such as a water feature, a planting bed, or a panoramic vista. Design your gazebo with the view in mind, elevating the floor to enhance a vantage point.

Consider the approach to your gazebo as well. If it's in the midst of an expanse of lawn, no path may be necessary. But if it's tucked among plantings, install a walkway. Choose path materials that complement the gazebo's style and surrounding plantings. Use decking to connect a gazebo to a patio or to your house.

easy transition

above right: **This gazebo extends over the edge of a pond and uses concrete piers for support and decking for flooring. Simple furnishings, including a hammock chair and canvas deck chairs, suit the retreat's casual theme. The design works as a transition into the landscape.**

capture attention

right: **A gazebo can serve as a focal point, even in a small yard. This backyard boasts an eye-grabbing feature: a hill. The addition of this elegantly contoured gazebo embellishes an attractive scene. Citrus trees adorn the slope and provide a solid green backdrop to the gazebo; a profusion of roses and perennials envelopes the structure with color.**

modern art

left: **A nontraditional gazebo design aims for a playful or flamboyant effect rather than matching the house. A table and chairs tucked inside the hideaway provide a refreshing perch for viewing the surrounding wildflowers. The gazebo's height draws eyes through the meadow planting, forming an effective focal point. Slatted sides cast ample shade for garden visitors.**

gazebos: metal

romantic retreat

You need not travel to far-flung places to enjoy the experience of an intimate getaway when you plan a patio retreat that overflows with classic appeal. A wrought-iron gazebo (*right*) assembles easily from a kit. It adorns a backyard with the look of a formal English structure and the feel of a romantic fantasy. The retreat took root on a boring concrete slab, transforming an abandoned patio into an outdoor destination.

Pea gravel spread on top of the concrete yields a new look without any digging, jackhammering, or staining. Redwood bender board secured by stakes keeps the gravel from spilling into the surrounding lawn. Wrought-iron and rattan furnishings equip the gazebo with the necessities for outdoor dining. Natural-hue serving pieces and linens transform everyday meals and snacks into special-occasion fare. Wrought-iron candleholders flank the gazebo's entryway.

Generous containers anchor the four corners of the gazebo with rounded lines that echo the curving wrought-iron structure. Tropical mandevilla vines twine up the gazebo's arched sides. In regions with harsh winters, plant hardy vines, such as climbing roses, trumpet vine, or wisteria, directly into the ground at the base of the gazebo. Use containers near the vines, filling them to overflowing with colorful annuals.

Washable mosquito netting drapes luxuriously over the 9½×7-foot-wide gazebo, softening the scene. The netting hangs from rings looped over the gazebo's ceiling hook.

outdoor dining

left: A gazebo furnished with a dining table and chairs allows for meals beneath the stars or for enjoying coffee while reading the morning newspaper. The table also offers a sturdy surface for playing board games, doing homework, or munching an after-school snack. Select accessories that complement the gazebo's style or material, if you like. In this case, wrought iron shapes the theme in furniture and candlestands as well as the overall structure.

123

gazebos: multipurpose

open-air oasis

A vine-covered gazebo blends family-friendly function into any backyard, no matter the size. The one shown *right* and *opposite* serves year-round outdoor living. It provides a family dining room or sleeps as many as six kids for a slumber party. The gazebo also serves as a meeting room. Design your gazebo to suit your garden lifestyle. Begin with a simple hexagonal shape set on concrete piers to lift the floor above ground level.

plush palace

above right: Lush morning glories cover the gazebo with living color.

fresh-air fare

right: Steps provide extra seating and ample space for container gardens.

weekend luxury

Dress your gazebo for outdoor dining during the week with a table and chairs, but on the weekend outfit it for leisurely living with a foam mattress cut to fit the floor dimensions. Use weather-worthy fabric to upholster a 4-inch-thick round mattress and add sham-covered bed pillows. Enjoy your gazebo as a fresh-air family room with plenty of space for casual conversation, reading, and napping.

comfort zone

left: **A foam mattress and plenty of throw pillows make a lounge-friendly family room. This 7½×7-foot redwood-and-cedar structure features stepped sides topped with a ledge that serves as a backrest and a place to set refreshments.**

125

tepees

native heritage

In today's garden, a tepee offers a simple but effective structure, providing height in otherwise flat planting schemes and forming a shelter that's affordable and easy to build. Tepees work well in children's gardens, creating small spaces for big imaginations to weave adventures.

To construct a retreat replete with adventure and fun, start with 6- to 8-foot poles, such as metal reinforcing rods, saplings, or bamboo. Lash the poles together at least 6 inches from their top ends, then spread the free ends away from one another, creating a circular shape. Position the poles to form a distinct entrance. Anchor your

powwow playhouse

below: **Branches form a tepee that's too pretty to cover with vines. Stock the tepee with child-size chairs, and it will certainly provide allure.**

structure to the ground by pushing the poles 6 to 12 inches into the soil. Use hollow-style post anchors to secure saplings in place. Have children plant pole beans near the base of each support. Teach kids how to tell when beans are ripe, and you'll have them eating their vegetables in no time.

For more garden building projects, visit **www.bhg.com/ bkgardenprojects**.

tip-top tepee

left: **Design a vine-entwined dining room courtesy of a metal reinforcing rod tepee and easy-to-grow morning glories. Each of the four 10-foot-tall rods rises from the corner of a plank-enclosed mulch floor. The tops of the rods are lashed securely with wire and topped with a metal fence-post finial. A classic bistro-style table and chairs fit neatly inside the tepee.**

127

rooms with a purpose

Well-planned garden rooms provide places for you to live comfortably and to manage the necessary details of daily life. Rooms also separate outdoor living areas from functional but not-so-pretty spaces, such as a compost pile, the garbage can nook, or a stack of firewood. How you segue from hardworking areas to garden hideaways depends on your personal tastes and your family's needs.

making room Extend your home's living space into the garden by making outdoor rooms for dining, sleeping, partying, bathing, and more. Turn your fantasies of a cozy, inviting retreat into real spaces that offer privacy, comfort, and your favorite amenities.

Involve everyone in your household in the process of planning an outdoor room. By incorporating elements that address divergent desires, such as places to eat, read, rest, play, and work, the room will be pleasing to everyone. With careful orchestration, you can design rooms around a highly specific use or multiple purposes.

focus on function The most inviting rooms ensure ease of enjoyment. So aim to arrange a traditional outdoor room, such as a family room, functional porch, or garden hideaway, with basic amenities: seating, lighting, and storage. Other essentials include easy access and maintenance, sources of water and electricity, and shelter from weather.

Just as you gather ideas from a garden tour, visit a gamut of garden rooms on the following pages and find inspiration. Room by room, page by page, discover building techniques, decorative details, and creative approaches to carving an expanse of your yard into a garden escape.

patios

problem solvers

Carving living space from a yard that's too small, too exposed, or too hilly is a challenge. But it also is an avenue for creativity. No matter how difficult your yard seems, adding a patio instantly opens up a realm of outdoor living possibilities.

Overcome a compact or narrow yard by slicing the space into smaller garden rooms *(below right)*. Use different flooring materials, such as brick, turf, and gravel, to outline the areas. In the end, you'll achieve a sense of spacious luxury. Add lush plantings to suggest an atmosphere of abundance.

If neighboring properties rub shoulders with yours, boost privacy with structural elements that establish seclusion, frame views, and provide more space for growing plants. A pergola offers shelter from glaring sun and blocks views from upper floors of nearby

architectural art
above: Add the curve and columns of a classic peristyle to open a small space, frame a view, and define an intimate room.

dynamic duo
right: A confined yard blooms into two spacious garden rooms, thanks to distinctive flooring and a transition area between the two rooms. Plantings direct traffic flow and views, overcoming the boxiness of the space.

homes. Add a peristyle *(opposite top)*, a curving structure borrowed from Greek architecture, to screen views. The elegant structure also creates an illusion of depth, which makes a small area appear larger. Wrap columns with climbing roses, which will cover the entire structure with easy beauty. Other good plant choices include wisteria, bittersweet, clematis, or Carolina jessamine.

downhill trickle

left: **Put a slope to work as a natural bed for a tumbling waterfall and stream. Place a brick-floor seating area at one end of the water feature; edge it with wet-loving plants.**

plan the perfect patio

You're more likely to use a garden room if it includes the elements you desire most. But you may not have identified those yet. Use these tips to determine what you want and how to get it:

- **dream a little:** Before you tear out that old patio or build a new one, think about how you want to use the space. If you plan to entertain, how many people could the area accommodate? Do you want the room to be open to the stars, drenched in sun, or protected from both?

- **take another look:** What do you see when you look at the patio area (existing or potential) from various rooms in the house? How could you improve the view year-round?

- **think outside the box:** If you have a sloping yard, put gravity to work and turn it into a trickling water feature. Include a small terrace with a seating area at the top of the watercourse. Plan a patio at the base of the stream and enjoy the full effect of the scene.

- **move it:** If you plan to acquire furniture for your outdoor room, consider pieces that could move indoors for off-season use.

yard *&* garden projects | **131**

patios: millstone fountain

cost	make it	skill
$$$	weekend	moderate

you will need

- shovel
- plastic tub (5-foot diameter, 18 inches deep)
- concrete pre-mix
- small submersible pump
- 28-inch plastic tube
- perforated 6-inch–diameter PVC pipe (20 inches long)
- three or four 6-inch–diameter PVC pipes (25 inches long)
- round river rock (1½– to 4-inch size)
- millstone (4-foot–diameter), or large, flat rock

makeover magic

What to do with a small, flat, and poorly draining site where grass struggles to grow? Compose a stylish garden room with a bluestone patio, woodland plantings that covet moist roots, and a millstone fountain gently spouting water.

This ground, now a room (*opposite*), supported a garage and driveway for 60 years. When these elements were removed and the soil was exposed, the yard became a mucky swamp. Adding sand and organic matter to the soil improved its drainage and fertility, but it took more than a few plantings to create a garden escape. A beautiful stone floor and comfortably functional table and chairs outfitted the room in purposeful style, but a focal point remained elusive. A millstone fountain solved the problem, adding instant drama and delight to the simple scene.

fountain artistry

right: A millstone-turned-fountain provides the focal point for a garden room. River rocks decorate the surface and perimeter of the fountain. It's also an ideal place for the rocks gathered on hikes or vacations.

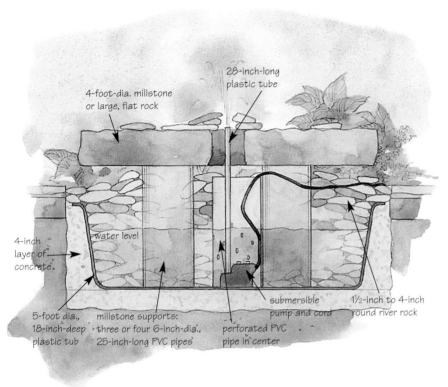

4-foot-dia. millstone or large, flat rock

28-inch-long plastic tube

4-inch layer of concrete

water level

5-foot dia., 18-inch-deep plastic tub

millstone supports: three or four 6-inch-dia., 25-inch-long PVC pipes

perforated PVC pipe in center

submersible pump and cord

1½-inch to 4-inch round river rock

Constructing a millstone fountain requires no special skills. Finding an authentic millstone (historically used for grinding grain) can be tricky. Alternatively, achieve the same effect by drilling a 4-inch-diameter hole in the center of a large, flat rock. Or drill a hole in the bottom of a big, low ceramic bowl to accommodate the fountain jet.

Prepare to install a millstone fountain by siting it near an outlet equipped with a ground fault circuit interrupter (GFCI); install a GFCI outlet if one doesn't exist. Excavate a hole to hold the plastic tub (water reservoir). Line the hole with a 4-inch-thick layer of concrete (made from concrete premix) for a sturdy base for the fountain. After several days, when the concrete has dried, insert the tub. The tub should sit level and flush with the ground. Add or remove soil until the area is level with the top edge of the tub.

Attach a fountain jet to a small submersible pump. Place the assembly inside a length of perforated PVC pipe. Position the pipe and pump on the bottom of the tub. Set up the millstone support PVC pipes. Fill in around these pipes with layers of round river rock, until the rocks are within an inch of the tops of the millstone support pipes. Fill the reservoir with water and connect the pump to your home's electrical source. Adjust the water flow of the pump to create the amount of bubble or spray desired. With strong helpers, position the millstone over the fountain jet. Top the stone and surround its perimeter with river rocks. Add water to the reservoir periodically to offset evaporation, especially during hot weather.

natural feel
left: The natural tones of a bluestone patio blend beautifully with surrounding plantings; the enticing setting entails little upkeep. The fountain imitates a bubbling woodland spring.

decks

free agents

When the scenery boasts beauty that begs for seating positioned to take in the view, opt for a freestanding deck. Construct it anywhere a patio would fit. Also choose decking to conquer problem areas. A deck tames a slope like nothing else, providing living space in an unused area. Terrace a deck along a hillside, perching it atop the peak or tucking it into a steep grade. Provide access with sturdy paths that are easy on your feet, such as large stepping-stones or more decking.

Your deck may need railings. For most communities, building codes require railings on decks that stand more than 30 inches off the ground. Check local ordinances to be sure your deck meets the code. If you can, leave the sides railing-free and nestle plantings along the deck's edge to make deck and surroundings one. Or edge the platform with benches instead of railings.

Add details, such as lighting or outdoor speakers, depending on how you intend to use the space. If you enjoy grilling and your deck is situated near the house, consider running a gas line to the outdoor room for greater ease in fueling your grill without the hassles of bottled gas.

showstopping scenery

right: **A freestanding deck with comfortable chairs and a lovely vista becomes a favorite place to gather with family and friends. Position the deck so you can enjoy the view every day. Add a table for dining, especially if your view includes sunrises or sunsets.**

decked out

left: **Decorate a spacious freestanding deck with container gardens, wind art, or statuary. Include a tabletop fountain to add the soothing sound of running water.**

decorative strategy

Furnish a freestanding deck with ensembles that suit the scene. A simple park-style bench affords ample seating. Provide a market umbrella if there are no trees to cast cooling shade. For an area you use infrequently, select sturdy metal or weather-resistant wooden seating. If your deck represents an outdoor family room, stock it with cushioned chairs and chaises. Include a table for eating and end tables to hold drinks. A coffee table encircled with a bench and chairs encourages conversation. If heavy winds sweep regularly across your deck, choose furniture that's weighty enough to withstand the blasts, or you'll be chasing chairs and tables across your yard. Built-in seating won't go astray. Consider using it for a deck positioned to capture views in a far-flung reach of your yard or to provide additional seating if you frequently entertain large numbers of guests.

decks: pergola topper

cost	make it	skill
$$$	4 days	moderate

you will need

eight 4×4 posts

concrete premix

two 4×8 side beams (20 feet, 6 inches long)

fourteen 4×4 truss tops (6 feet, 9 inches long); twenty-one 4×4 short truss pieces, seven 4×4 truss bottoms (9 feet long)

4×8 ridge beam (20 feet, 6 inches long)

galvanized deck screws

compound miter saw, drill

open-air room

Count on a deck to extend the comforts of your home past its walls. Customize the structure by adding architectural details, such as curved edges, multiple levels, or overhead beams.

Include gravity-defying furniture, such as hanging chairs, a swing, or a hammock. Add overhead support to suspend these footloose seats. Settle on a structural design that echoes the architectural elements of your house. Repeat rooflines, for instance.

This fresh-air family room (right) features a double-decker floor plan with a pergola, a boardwalk, and swinging chairs. To build this pergola, use pressure-treated wood for frames and posts; choose cedar for the other parts. Join all pieces with galvanized deck screws. Paint or stain the wood before constructing the pergola.

double-layer decking

right: **A deck that adjoins a home through wide-access doors extends indoor living spaces with impressive square footage.**

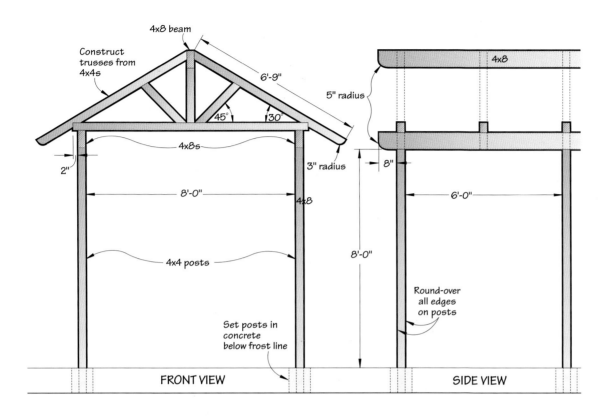

Construct trusses from 4x4s

4x8 beam

6'-9"

5" radius

45°   30°

4x8s

2"

3" radius

8'-0"

4x8

4x4 posts

Set posts in concrete below frost line

FRONT VIEW

4x8

8"

6'-0"

8'-0"

Round-over all edges on posts

SIDE VIEW

Dig postholes to just below the frost line. Insert the 4×4 posts and fill the holes with concrete. (Read about setting a post on page 85.)

Attach the two 4×8 side beams to the tops of the posts. Prebuild two trusses (from 4×4s) and have a friend help you mount one at the front and one at the rear of the structure, using galvanized deck screws. Then carefully lift the 4×8 ridge beam into place and screw the two trusses to it. Either prebuild the remaining five trusses and install each as a complete unit, or assemble them in place, one piece at a time.

If you wish, hang the chairs from the ridge beam, using eyebolts and swivel hooks.

deck extension

left: **A boardwalk topped with a pergola extends the deck into the garden. Hanging chairs provide breezy alternative seating to the formal furnishings in the outdoor family room on the deck.**

yard & garden projects | **137**

decks: stained rug

cost	make it	skill
$$	weekend	easy

you will need

deck cleaner and stiff brush

tape measure

T square and chalk line

utility knife

exterior-grade wood stain

tapered bristle brush

disposable sponge applicator

wooden retreat

Dress up the bare-board floors and railings of a deck with clever touches of color and creativity. Vintage porch molding brings ornate charm to the scene (*right*). Finials attached beneath house eaves, upside-down spandrels screwed atop deck rails, and salvage boards nailed to built-in seating suggest the look of an old-fashioned porch and add privacy. Large containers overflow with fast-growing annuals, forming a living screen.

Underfoot, a dull deck gives way to a custom area rug created with exterior stain. To make a similar floor, use an old bedsheet to help visualize the rug's size and shape; then on graph paper sketch to scale designs that suit your decorating strategy. A checkerboard pattern fits the cottage style of this haven. For a more formal look, try a double-bordered solid rug. Go for whimsy with curlicues and circles. Make a rug with hand (and paw) prints of family and friends.

magic carpet

right: **Roll out a colorful deck rug, courtesy of wood stain. A festive checkerboard design, made with two shades of exterior stain, transforms ordinary pressure-treated pine into a fanciful surface. Vintage wood details and window shutters assume new roles as deck railing and privacy screen. Bent willow furnishings complete the fashionable retreat.**

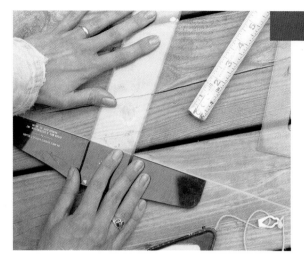

1 **clean and draw** Clean the wood using a deck cleaner and a stiff brush. Use a T square and chalk line to mark out the rug design. As you mark lines, step back and see if they appear straight or have someone help you ensure the lines are straight. Create stencils for intricate designs and trace them with chalk. The checkerboard rug is a 93-inch square composed of 15-inch squares framed by a 9-inch-wide border.

2 **score and stain** Score ¼-inch-deep design lines using a utility knife to prevent the stain from bleeding into adjacent areas. Scoring creates a thin well in which runoff stain will pool. Begin staining with the lightest color stain. Work your way from the center of the rug outward. Stain every other square, using a tapered bristle brush; a disposable sponge applicator makes straight edges. Let the stain dry completely, according to the manufacturer's directions. Fill in the remaining squares with a darker shade. Stain the border last.

knock on wood
Search for vintage woodwork trims at demolition sites, salvage yards, auctions, and antiques shops. Check for rot by pricking the wood with a penknife. Soft, spongy spots indicate a problem. Plan to remove and repair small rot patches with wood filler. Inspect bottom edges for warping. If the piece is suitable, buy it. New, machine-milled pine trim is affordable and develops a vintage look as it weathers.

rooftop room

sky-high sanctuary

Live large in the smallest yard by setting your sights high. Rooftop gardening opens a whole new arena for space-constrained gardeners. Rooms that give you a bird's-eye view of the ground promise privacy and afford ample planting areas.

Before building a rooftop garden room, consult with an architect or a structural engineer for advice on how to reinforce existing structures to accommodate the additional weight of raised planting beds and decking. Plan to site heavy items, such as planters, near the edges of your skyscraping room. Choose lightweight materials, such as fiberglass, plastic, resin, and PVC, for furniture, pots, and even decking materials. Include electrical outlets and water spigots in your rooftop room.

Lay deck planks over existing roofing. Screw instead of nail decking down to allow raising the deck for roof repairs. Enclose your room's perimeter with waist-high planters, built-in benches, or lattice walls. Lattice panels weigh less than a solid wall and let the breezes blow through.

Plan your rooftop room with convenience and comfort in mind. Include easy access to your sky-high getaway, providing more than one entry/exit if possible. Build a small landing on a steep staircase to make the ascent and descent easier. Edge the landing deck with potted flowers for color.

Arrange comfortable furniture in your room, and add a canopy or an umbrella for protection from glaring sun or drenching rain.

high-rise garden
left: For gardeners with heavily shaded beds at ground level, a rooftop garden opens possibilities to grow sun-loving plants. Select drought-tolerant bloomers that stand up to wind and sun, such as marigold, coreopsis, calendula, golden marguerite, and sunflowers. Include a small tree, such as a Japanese maple, in a pot. Incorporate water-retentive crystals into soil in planters to minimize watering chores.

living rooms

family central

This house-hugging addition transformed a steep, unused backyard into a family-focused room with all the perks of a luxury vacation. A sunny area for dining and barbecuing occupies one end of the deck, a vine-smothered arbor beckons with cooling shade at the other end, and a sunken spa bubbles in between. The three areas add up to an outdoor family room and entertainment center that has become the heart of the home.

classical tradition

right: The classic design of deck-railing details complements the traditional-style house. The deck's middle section drops down to an inviting spa area. Lower railings near the spa permit an unhindered view from inside the kitchen.

Redwood decking and white railings create a clean look that complements the house. Marble-composite columns hold the arbor aloft with architectural finesse and promise a longer life than wood. Barefoot-friendly redwood resists cracking; it doesn't require headed nails, which cause hot spots. Easy-to-clean white resin furniture and cushions provide casual elegance for entertaining.

The spa offers year-round enjoyment. A peaked arbor over the main deck room features a dense cover of vines and a ceiling fan. A 48-inch square of glass ceiling fits into the arbor's peak and protects the fan from above. A ceiling fan lowers the temperature in the vine-canopied room 8 to 10 degrees.

family-friendly features

- Build multiple levels. Give kids their own play area, such as a sandbox or patio adjacent to a deck.

- Include a toy-storage area for the kids to store their stuff. Tuck a storage shed for large toys under the deck.

- Plan for safety. Top the spa with a lockable safety cover. Keep the spa's water temperature less than 104° F.

- Opt for wide steps. Two-foot-wide stairs prove toddler negotiable and provide extra seating. They also offer room for pots of herbs for grilling, salads, or drinks.

natural cooling

left: A double-top arbor boasts cool shade in the living room beneath it and easy care. The unfinished top layer of the ceiling supports wisteria and trumpet vines. The lower structure holds a ceiling fan.

dining rooms

set the mood

Mealtime takes on a new dimension when it's accompanied by birdsong or a starry night. Simple touches in your outdoor dining room are sure to heighten the festive mood and make conversation sparkle and the food taste better.

Load a welcoming side table with beverages, a variety of glasses, a corkscrew, plenty of ice, and cocktail napkins. Arrange chairs, benches, and small tables in comfortable groupings to encourage mingling.

Set a table that's garden-fresh looking and inviting. A centerpiece of flowers adds instant charm. Make either a low arrangement or one of extra-long stems in a tall vase that won't interfere with conversing. Float individual blooms in glass bowls for place-setting pizzazz. Or sprinkle flower petals on the table just before guests arrive.

aegean style

above: Host a Mediterranean-style dinner by using white linens, pots full of bright red geraniums, lots of fresh fruit and cheese, and flickering lantern light.

buffet bench

right: Press traditional garden gear into fancifully functional dining roles. Use a potting bench as a stylish buffet or use a wheelbarrow as an ice chest.

Gather sprigs of fresh herbs into small bouquets tied with raffia; set a bouquet at each place setting as a fragrant party favor.

Extend the garden theme with lightweight, terra-cotta-look containers as serving pieces for ice, bottled drinks, salad, bread, and such. Available in a variety of sizes, shapes, and styles, the classy-looking styrene pots come without drainage holes and won't chip, crack, or break.

Light the night with candles, twinkle lights strung through trees and shrubs, and lanterns. Include relaxing sounds in your outdoor decor scheme, such as a trickling fountain or soft music.

simple decor
left: Cushioned chairs, a fabric-covered table, and a sisal rug help turn an old shed into a cozy room for coffee or tea. A vintage chandelier makes a perfect candelabra.

145

dining rooms: pavilion

pavilion pleasures

In many cases, the first room that sprouts in the
garden is a dining room. A dining area needs no
more than a table and chairs to dress the space
in simple or elegant style. If you entertain often
or want to enjoy alfresco meals on a regular basis,
consider adding an overhead structure, walls, or
flooring to set the room apart. Of course, it's easiest
to set up a dining area on an existing deck or
patio. A pergola or an overhanging tree provides
ample covering to create a sense of place. For the
serious entertainer, a dining pavilion (*right* and
below) may be in order.

This 8×20-foot latticework wonder offers
a sheltered, comfortable place for a dozen or
more friends to gather and linger over food
and conversation. A generous table and a mix
of folding chairs easily fit the space. Draped folds

natural air-conditioning

below: **Various openings in the lath structure
contribute to circulation through this fresh-air
dining room. The design features include large
stair-step-cutout doorways in the pavilion's
front, windows in the back that swing open
or latch shut, and 8-foot-wide open ends.**

of weatherproof fabric provide softness and privacy, evoking visions of Tuscany or Provence. Soft electric lighting gently brightens the nighttime scene.

Construct your pavilion with weather-worthy materials. Plastic lath walls create privacy, permit air movement, and conjure an illusion of spaciousness in the narrow area. Underfoot, vinyl plank flooring provides a surface that's sturdy and care free.

The matching pedestals outside the structure continue the formal design with plastic lath that never needs painting. The urn-topped pedestals extend the pavilion's welcoming aura. Foliage tapestries skirt the doorways with the jewel tones of coleus, plectranthus, and sweet potato vine.

have a seat

Outdoor dining lends itself to lingering for hours, so cater to comfort in your seating.

- Add cushions covered in weather-resistant fabrics to soften hard seats.

- Choose lightweight pieces, such as plastic or canvas chairs, for easy mobility.

- Mix and match styles, choosing chairs in either the same color scheme or made from the same materials.

- Consider storage options. Folding chairs take up a minimum of storage space. Stackable resin seats also store easily.

common thread

left: Plastic lath weaves a unifying architectural theme throughout this garden, from pedestals and dining room walls to garden tool storage, fencing, screens, and accents. The white lath suits the formal look, whereas a wood tone would appear more rustic.

sleeping rooms

sweet dreams

Once a part of life on sultry summer nights, especially in the South, the sleeping porch offers a dreamy setting where the music of nature lulls you to sleep and nudges you awake.

A screened porch begs to be enjoyed, with its breeze-friendly walls and sometimes-shady, sometimes-sunny scenery. If your home doesn't include a porch, you have options. Settle a comfortable old sofa on a covered patio or hang a hammock under a balcony. Wherever a roof and a wall meet, there's potential for a sleeping room.

outdoor ease

right: Creature comforts complete a room designed for rest. Drape a sofa with a matelassé spread, a snuggly throw, and big pillows— naptime awaits.

Select furniture that caters to relaxation and rest. Choose a bed based on its functionality and your budget. A daybed, for instance, doubles as seating. Cart a lightweight futon outdoors to make a chaise for two. Recycle a sofa bed that's perfectly comfortable but benefits from a slipcover.

Nothing says take a break better than a hammock, whether it's dangling from a ceiling or perched in an iron stand. Suspend your hammock in a spot with plenty of swinging room. To hang a hammock, choose heavy-duty eyebolts and chain; screw hooks securely into ceiling joists, posts, or wall studs.

breezy bed
below: Adopt tropical-isle style to create a room that's big on comfort, color, and seaside charm. Choose a scheme that relies on this trio of materials to make decorating a snap: canvas, rattan, and wicker.

meditation rooms

peaceful escape

In a world of haste and hassle, your garden offers a place to unwind, find peace of mind, and restore your sensibilities. Tend your garden as a sanctuary for your soul and it will provide you with a place to sit back, relax, breathe deeply, rest, and rejuvenate.

Whereas gardening encourages healthy exercise and provides plenty of fresh air and sunshine, connecting with nature calms the mind. Just as a garden represents a spiritual haven for many, you can create a refuge in your yard to suit your vision of paradise. Call it your yoga garden, the reading room, your pondering place, or whatever. A garden sanctuary includes basic elements, whether you desire seclusion, quiet, solitude, or a place to sit and watch the birds.

Begin by closing your eyes and imagining yourself in this restful place. Then find a spot for

a place for repose

Every garden contains the building blocks of a meditative escape.

- **conceal and heal:** Partially enclose an existing seating area to foster solitude. Silence soothes the soul.

- **putter and ponder:** Find refreshment in basic gardening activities. Let weeding, digging, and planting relax your mind.

- **rest and refuel:** A rocking chair, a swing, or a hammock has soothing appeal.

- **naturalize and nurture:** Commune with nature's beauty and peace via simple building materials: stone, wood, bamboo, and clay.

take a break

right: A garden that fosters relaxation and serenity includes a sheltered place to sit. From here, you can look out and see what's beautiful about your garden (instead of focusing on what needs to be done).

your garden escape: under a tree or tucked into a secluded corner, a place protected from wind that captures sunshine in winter and shade in summer. Choose shrubs or a structure to shape a secluded room, hidden from view of the house and from nearby traffic.

What do you need to relax? Soft plants, fragrant herbs, and pastel blooms cater to the senses. Do you prefer tinkling bells, a wind chime, a creaking windmill, or silence? Would a water feature rest your mind? Consider adding a lily pond or a still, shallow pool that inspires reflection.

year-round retreat
left: An enclosed meditation room sits in a quiet corner of the garden, offering a delightful haven for contemplation. The folding doors open wide enough to blur the line between the room and outside.

151

meditation rooms

worlds apart
Find sanctuary in your garden by designing a room that will rejuvenate and refresh. Any garden can become a peaceful haven when furnishings include the following:

entry Use an arbor, an arch, or a gate to mark the threshold to your special place. Create a welcoming ambience with a climbing rose, a sign, or a bell.

seating A bench, a reclining chaise, or a bed invites you to stretch out or put up your feet. A cushioned seat with a backrest proves restful. Plant a soft, mossy rug to lie upon.

viewing platform
right: Reed matting from a home improvement store, bamboo poles, and a beach-combed dock panel outfit a room for garden contemplation. Embroidered pillows and a cotton throw soften the seating. Mosquito netting comes in handy too.

low maintenance Set up plantings, including those in containers, with a regular supply of water from drip irrigation automated with a timer. Construct a handy place to store cushions, candles, and other accessories for your haven.

restful oasis

left: Still or moving, water brings a reflective element to any garden. A few floating blooms in a lotus bowl, believed by Hindus to inspire tranquillity and help purify the spirit, reflect nature's beauty and peace.

artful inspiration

left: A patterned pebble mosaic engages the mind in thoughtful reverie. Gather stones at a quarry or rock yard. Sort stones by size, shape, and color. Practice laying stones in patterns on a flat surface. Frame the area with edging. Set stones at ground level in 1 inch of mortar on a 2-inch base of sand and crushed rock. Work quickly and in small sections, because mortar sets within minutes.

bathing rooms

shower power

An outdoor shower or bath proves cool, convenient, and decadently refreshing as it washes away the effects of toiling in the garden. Site a shower in a private alcove behind shrubbery or walls. This bathing room (*right*) sequesters a shower with recycled boards. Salvaged cupboards, a stone floor, and secondhand furnishings complete the room. The rustic ambience enhances the delight of bathing beneath the sun or moon. Cover a shower with rafters and plant vines to cloak them if the stall is visible from above.

shower amenities

right: Burlap curtains add privacy; a cupboard keeps soap, shampoo, and towels handy. A potted gardenia scents the air.

summer showers

left: Locate a shower in a sunny place and enjoy the warmth while you bathe. Either build the enclosure or install a prefabricated unit. Incorporate nonslip flooring of wood decking or flagstone. Interplant stones or pavers with creeping mint or thyme.

let it pour

You'll be set to get wet when you add a shower to your garden.

- Construct an enclosure on the side of an existing building, such as a garage, a potting shed, or a storage building. Guarantee privacy with sidewalls and a door or dense shrubbery.

- Build waterproof walls of vinyl planking or lattice. If you prefer wood, choose rot-resistant lumber, such as cedar. Seal wood with a water-repellant preservative.

- In cold-winter regions, include a valve to permit draining the plumbing and turning off the water supply (to prevent rupturing frozen pipes) in late fall.

- A portable camper shower is a snap to install. Look for solar-heated models to ensure warm water.

bathing rooms

bathroom decor

Imagine soaking in a warm, bubbly tub in shimmery sunshine or under sparkly stars. As a place for luxury and pleasure, the bathing garden is an ancient concept with recently renewed appeal. A bath soothes the mind as well as the muscles.

Create an outdoor bathing room with a tub for soaking. Save a claw-footed tub from a remodeling project or acquire one at a salvage store. Fill the tub using a bucket or a hose; let cool water sit in the sun until it's warm enough for a bath. Or have a plumber connect your outdoor tub or shower to indoor hot water. Warm water soothes; cool water exhilarates.

Furnish your bathing room with convenience, comfort, and pleasure in mind. A plant stand forms a handy towel rack. A small table or stool holds a refreshing drink for sipping while bathing. Fill a basket full of your favorite bathtime necessities: soap, essential oils, a loofah sponge, scented candles, a favorite book or magazine, and thick towels.

For more stylish gardening ideas, visit **www.bhg.com/bkgarden**.

earthly delights

Grow a garden that's ripe with plants renowned as boons to bathing. Gather leaves or blossoms, fresh or dried, into a muslin or cheesecloth bag. Tie the bag closed with cotton string. Float the bag in bathwater or hang it under the faucet while filling the tub. Float additional leaves or flowers on bathwater.

- **soothing:** lavender, chamomile flowers, lemon balm

- **stimulating:** peppermint, rosemary, spearmint, anise hyssop

- **therapeutic:** sage, rosemary, peppermint, eucalyptus, thyme

- **romantic:** rose petals, calendula petals, jasmine flowers, gardenia flowers

private oasis

left: Soothe the senses with a relaxing outdoor bath tucked into a secluded part of your garden, sheltered by shrubs or other tall plants or enclosed by walls. Build a screen of lattice, bamboo, reed, or fabric for more privacy. Train vines on trellises to make living curtains; choose fragrant flowering plants, such as jasmine or a climbing rose.

the working garden

The best, most functional elements in your garden work hard and look good. Decorative elements often prove practical and even provide solutions. A handsome potting shed that stands as an impressive focal point in the garden also houses tools and serves as a handy entertainment center in a small backyard. A garden that is both beautiful and functional will multiply your pleasure.

hardworking decor Examine your garden's decorative potential from a practical point of view. Consider necessities such as pathways, seating, and storage. See how stepping–stones (especially when beautifully crafted and creatively placed) entice you and visitors to enter and explore the garden with greater anticipation. Turn a needed storage place for tools into a piece of garden art that keeps your gear within easy reach.

Each element of your garden decor should earn its keep, whether it provides comfort and efficiency or gives you a place to stash furniture cushions out of the rain.

rewards for creativity Drum up your creative energy and transform scraps of wood into unique houses or feeders that attract birds; turn old glass mixing bowls into classy cloches; or make shapely garden edgers with ordinary terra–cotta floor tiles.

Heighten the satisfaction you feel in your garden by building a seating ensemble designed for durability and multiple uses. If you've always dreamed of a place that would help organize your pots and garden gadgets but have no room for a shed, devise a potting bench that doubles as an elegant buffet.

paths

from the ground up

Once you decide to construct a path, create one that will be easy on the eye, the feet, and the budget. Focus on intended use and maintenance when selecting the path's surface. Gravel and mulch, although inexpensive, must be renewed every few years.

Gravel promises a crunch underfoot; mulch provides a cushioned walk. Flagstone dishes up durability that can't be beat, but it can be expensive and it's slippery when wet. Work small sections of flagstone into paths. Brick and clay pavers, which are durable and relatively easy to lay, inspire creative patterns. Choose bricks and pavers rated climate-tolerant for your region. Concrete and concrete pavers withstand any climate. For large projects, concrete pavers can be pricey, but interlocking types make installation easy.

country charm
above right: **Flagstones and bricks lend your pathways old-world enchantment.**

reward wanderers
right: **Focal points, such as benches or arbors, along your path will woo walkers.**

formal footpath
far right: **Economical landscape timbers set in the ground border a path of square stepping-stones and gravel.**

piecing it all together

Planning a path includes a vital decision: What surface or building material to use. Take into account your budget, the amount of labor you're willing to invest, and the style of path you desire. In general, the more formal a path, the more expensive and time-consuming it is to build. Note: the following costs are approximate and subject to change.

The most popular footings for garden paths are decomposed granite and tumbled stones. Hot choices for garden paths include:

1 **Arizona flagstone:**
$239 per ton

2 **tumbled Connecticut bluestone:**
$475 per ton

3 **decomposed granite:** $50 per ton

4 **Three Rivers flagstone:** $415 per ton

5 **concrete brick:** 50 cents each

6 **black slate:** $475 per ton

7 **eucalyptus mulch:**
$3.99 per 20-pound bag

8 **Connecticut bluestone:**
$445 per ton

9 **burgundy clay brick:**
90 cents each

10 **cedar 2×4:**
$8 for 12-foot board

11 **tumbled Connecticut bluestone:**
$475 per ton

12 **pea gravel:** $2 for 50 pounds

13 **klinker brick:** 80 cents each

14 **gold quartzite:**
$250–$300 per ton

15 **Iron Mountain flagstone:**
$290 per ton

flower swirl

above: Flagstones arranged in a staggered pattern set the tone for this easygoing garden. Ruffles of sweet alyssum soften the stones' edges. Positioning pavers in a purposefully casual, meandering line adds visual dimension to small spaces.

stepping-stones

trailblazing tips

The best garden pathways lead through hidden
nooks and create a special effect too. Stepping-stones
blaze the way as the simplest of paths. Designing
paths is fun; building them, though also fun, is
work. Tailor the amount of heave-ho according to
your choice of path-making materials. Flagstones
set among established plantings make for less
work than a neatly edged path of carefully
patterned pavers.

   Stepping-stones offer a comfortable, appealing
way to guide visitors through a garden. Use
steppers for areas that are too difficult to mow or
surrounded by established plantings. To set stones

walk this way
right: **For a passage that's bordered with lush
plantings, devise a path that's equally eye-
catching to keep vision and feet moving along.**

fanciful footing
below: **Hand-cast your own whimsical steppers
such as these, made with imprints of large
rhubarb leaves on poured concrete forms.**

in the ground, excavate a shape equal to the stone's dimensions plus ½ inch deeper. Cover the bottom of the excavation with pea gravel ½ inch deep to allow drainage. Position the stone on top of the gravel, adding or removing soil to make it level. Tamp soil around the stone. If you are planting groundcovers as part of a path, keep plants well-watered the first growing season so that roots become well established.

Involve the whole family in pathway construction. Set pavers in nontraditional configurations. Create designs on paper or with the actual stones on your driveway before breaking ground.

Don't forget night lighting. Paths that provide access to important parts of your yard should be well-lit at night. Low-voltage lighting provides the best illumination.

flagstones go formal
above: Blue slate slabs roll out a welcome that's as formal as a black-tie affair, especially when evenly spaced and framed with neatly manicured grass. Edge a grass-and-stone walkway with bricks to make maintenance easier by giving mower wheels a place to roll without damaging nearby plantings.

a step apart
left: Surround steppers with earth-hugging plants for a natural effect. Mosses, creeping mint, blue star creeper, or creeping thyme fill gaps with ease.

yard & garden projects | **163**

stepping-stones: mosaic

cost	make it	skill
$	weekend	easy

you will need

- ceramic tiles or plates
- safety glasses
- hammer or tile nippers
- plain precast concrete stepping-stone
- thin-set mortar
- heavy rubber gloves
- large buckets or plastic bins
- ³⁄₁₆-inch notched trowel
- poly-blend sanded tile grout
- trowel or large rubber spatula
- sponge
- soft cloth

art underfoot

Handmade stepping-stones add an element of signature artwork to the garden without costing a mint. Make our mosaic steppers easily and as artfully as you wish. Design stones in one color scheme, as shown (*right*), or blend a kaleidoscope of hues.

Start with simple precast concrete stepping-stones and decorate with broken flea-market plates, scrap or discounted tiles, marbles, pebbles, shells, or recycled colored glass. If you avoid sharp plate pieces or tile shards, this is an ideal project to do with children. Place tiles or plates in a shallow box and cover with a cloth to prevent shards from flying. Wearing safety glasses, crack the plates and tiles into large pieces with a hammer or tile nippers. Use care: you want shards, not smithereens.

tiptoe stepping-stones

right: Stones made from pieced tile and broken plates may become slippery when wet. Use caution when walking on them after watering or rainstorms, or on dewy mornings. Surround steppers with gravel or decomposed granite to improve tread traction.

preparation Immerse the concrete **1**
stepping-stone in water; wet it thoroughly.
Prepare mortar following package directions,
aiming for a consistency of thin peanut
butter. Use a notched trowel to spread
a ¼- to ½-inch layer of mortar onto part
of the stone.

artistry Arrange mosaic pieces to suit **2**
your fancy, pressing them lightly into the
mortar. Work your way across the stone. Add
mortar as needed. Slather it beneath thinner
pieces to keep the surface even. Press pieces
level but not flush; leave crevices for grout.
When the surface is covered, clean any excess
mortar. Let the stone sit overnight.

sealing Prepare grout according to **3**
package directions. Scoop a large blob onto
the stone. Use a trowel or spatula to spread
the grout, pressing it into crevices, removing
excess as you go. Add more as needed.
Smooth a layer of grout or mortar on the
sides of the stone.

clean up When the grout sets (within **4**
minutes), use a wet sponge to wipe excess
grout from the sides of the stepper and the
top, rinsing the sponge often; wipe in both
directions. Repeat this process until the
surface is clean and fairly even; avoid
removing grout from the crevices. Let the
stone dry 24 to 48 hours, then buff it with
a soft cloth.

edging

framing a garden

Ideally, edging should go in first, before plants, but incorporating edging into existing gardens is also possible. Use it to corral chaos, to keep things neat and tidy. But it can be beautiful as well as functional. Choose edging material to complement plantings, not compete with them. Edgings can be changed over time as long as they aren't set in concrete.

If grass borders your beds, select edging that gives your mower room to roll, or you'll be weed-whacking around every planting bed. Raised edging is charming. Three inches is eye-pleasing; 10 to 12 inches provides the right height for sitting. To groom a living edge, use low-growing flowers or herbs, such as sedum, catmint, or thyme.

collector's dream

right: If you have a collection of shells, put them to work as edging by placing them upended or laid flat.

angled for distinction

below: Create a classic brick edge by digging a trench 4 to 5 inches deep. Add an inch of sand. Angle bricks into the sand, positioning half the brick above ground and half below.

triple-edge bed

left: A gardener's itch for increased bed space can mean moving edging outward. The edging in this bed began with rounded river rock, but then an extension of creeping thyme was added. Curved metal bands came later to help separate the plants from the adjacent mulch path.

secondhand surroundings

Even the most expensive garden implements suffer damage over time. Instead of tossing your trusty tools, use them as garden sentinels, edging your favorite plantings. Cut broken tool handles to a length of 8 inches or less. Place them into the soil, blade points up. Other fun edgings: On-edge broken clay saucers or plates, upside-down terra-cotta pots (4- to 6-inch diameter, painted brightly), or upside-down wine bottles dug into the soil.

edging: terra-cotta tile

cost	make it	skill
$–$$	weekend	moderate

you will need

- 12×12-inch terra-cotta floor tiles, ½ inch thick
- jigsaw and tile blade
- dust mask
- safety goggles
- mattock, spade, square-point shovel, or trowel
- foundation sealer
- bucket
- mulch (chopped bark or gravel)

border treatment

Edging treatments are limited only by a gardener's imagination. Whether you use prefabricated edging or craft your own bed borders, you'll discover that edging, like fences, makes for good neighbors.

Our edging project begins with terra-cotta floor or quarry tiles, cut to a pattern, and tucked into soil. The tiles help foster a microclimate around plants, retaining the sun's heat near roots and promoting lusher, bigger plants.

English gardeners favor a trench edging for segregating lawn and flowers. Use this method along the front of a tile edge to make a mowing strip. Using a sharp square-point shovel or spade, dig 4 to 6 inches into the sod. Lift out the turf, roots and all. Clean the trench thoroughly by hand, removing rocks and roots, then backfill with mulch (chopped bark or gravel).

tiling the garden

right: **Incorporate floor tiles into the garden as bed edging. Cut to suit your fancy, and turned on end, tiles keep turfgrass from invading flower beds.**

1 **cut** Measure your garden beds and calculate how many tiles you'll need, based on using 12-inch-square floor tiles. On tile-size paper, design a pattern, favoring simple, fluid lines. Trace the pattern onto tiles using a pencil. Use a jigsaw blade designed for cutting tile to trim tiles into shape; wear a dust mask and safety goggles. If trimming tiles is beyond your confidence level, hire out the job. If you want to tackle cutting tiles but don't own a jigsaw, rent or borrow one.

2 **position** Dip the lower 4 inches of cut tiles into a bucket of foundation sealer to help prevent the porous edges from crumbling. Let tiles dry overnight. Use a mattock, square-point shovel, or trowel to excavate a trench for the tiles. Dig a trench 4 inches deep and 1 inch wide. Remove sod, roots, and rocks. Stand tiles side by side in the trench. Backfill to hold them securely in place.

3 **corner** Traditional edging keeps plants in bounds, but you can also use the technique to create a raised bed called a strawberry collar, which helps keep delicate fruits off the ground and makes them easier to pick. Dig a 4-inch-deep trench and set in cut tiles, securing them in place with soil. Add amendments 2 to 3 inches deep to build up the soil inside. For a permanent collar, mortar the tile corners and seams together.

yard & garden projects **169**

furnishings

seating options

Select furniture for your garden the same way you would for your home. Choose pieces that suit your taste, your budget, and your garden's style, as well as those that offer durability. Your outdoor furniture must contend with weather sometimes at its fiercest, so buy the best you can afford. Start with one piece or complete an ensemble, keeping use in mind. If you entertain frequently, add pieces that complement a dining arrangement, such as a buffet or tea cart. If you just want a place to perch between weedings, an informal bench will do. Choose lightweight pieces if they'll be sitting in grass and must be moved for mowing. Furniture with classic lines easily overwinters in a sunroom or family room.

armchair gardener
right: **Brighten the lawn, deck, or patio with a cheery crop of flowers hand-painted on chair slats.**

eye-pleasing pair
below: **Group garden furniture of the same material. A rustic table and chair blend well with a formal bench because they're all made of wood.**

artistry unleashed

Turn your passion for posies into personalized seating with a few floral stencils, acrylic paint, and polyurethane sealant (*opposite*). Hand-paint original designs on wooden seats, or use stencils to get the look you want. The chair shown is outlined in green to suggest flower stems. A dry brush dipped in blue paint and patted on the surface creates a shaded look around the blooms.

To forgo fanciful flowers and simply paint wooden furniture, use exterior-grade latex. Rag-wipe wet paint to give it an instantly weathered look, or rag-wipe one color over another dry color to add even more interest. Seal with polyurethane finish, unless you want the chair to weather and peel (this process also occurs with a seal; it just takes longer). Check the finish each fall before storing furniture; reseal as necessary.

fabric finesse

Cushions made from fade-proof, outdoor-type fabrics resist stains, moisture, and mildew. Unlike vinyl, these fabrics breathe and feel cool to the touch, even beneath a searing summer sun. Always bring in pillows that aren't weather-resistant; morning dew can ruin a favorite cushion.

lounge lizard
above: Weeding can wait when a luxuriously cushioned lounge chair next to a lazy pond beckons. This vintage 1940s lounge exudes old-fashioned charm. Keep the period ambience with cushions made from vintage fabric.

hard as a rock
left: A stone-enclosed corner and bench become a cozy getaway with the addition of comfy pillows. Choose heavy linen slipcovers that remove easily for laundering.

furnishings

outdoor living

A gathering of furniture makes a garden more
of an outdoor living space. When choosing
furnishings, consider style, construction material
(wood, metal, or plastic), and number of
pieces. Wooden furniture offers durability and
affordability. Consider building your own or
hiring a local carpenter to craft pieces for you.
Here are some reasons to construct or customize
your own furniture grouping:

custom designs Building your own furniture,
using plans drawn up by master crafters or artists,
means your ensemble will be unique to you.

affordability Choosing top-of-the-line materials
to construct your furniture will help ensure its
durability. You can select fabric and make your
own cushions or have them made.

matching colors Stain or paint your furniture
in hues that complement and enhance your
garden. Instead of an off-the-shelf red, try
matching the blushing petals of your favorite lily.

ownership Building your own furniture
multiplies your sense of ownership in the outdoor
space you call home. A deeply satisfying sense of
pride comes with seeing your handmade creation.

cottage casual

right: Simple lines highlight cottage style, and
nowhere is that look more classically captured
than in an ensemble of Adirondack-inspired
furniture. An Adirondack chair offers roomy
armrests and spacious seating; a tray table
offers flexibility, with its detachable trays.
A low table doubles as a footrest with hidden
storage. To learn how to build this classic trio,
turn the page.

cost	make it	skill
$$	weekend	advanced

you will need

- one 4×8-foot sheet of ⅜-inch beadboard
- ¾-inch pine lumber (23 feet total)
- 1×2 (7 feet)
- table saw with dado blades
- table router with ⅜-inch straight bit
- jigsaw
- clamps
- masking tape
- pencil
- exterior-grade construction adhesive
- 1½- to 2-inch flathead phillips screws
- cordless drill
- bit for no. 8 screws
- ⅜-inch bit for plugs
- ⅜-inch flathead taper plugs
- ⅜-inch wood dowels

build a chair

Beadboard paneling adds to this chair's stylish look. Use ¾-inch pine lumber for frame pieces; ⅜-inch beadboard wainscoting for panels. Begin by drawing patterns (*below right*) on lumber. Use a table jigsaw to cut two of everything on the pattern grid except for piece A. Label all pieces using masking tape and a pencil.

Join pieces using weatherproof glue and screws. Use 1½- to 2-inch flathead phillips screws except where noted. Throughout assembly, countersink screws that would be visible and fill holes with ⅜-inch flathead taper plugs.

Starting with the chair back, use a dado blade to cut a ⅜×⅜-inch groove into pieces A, B, and D. Join side pieces (B) to the top of the back (A). Apply glue to the grooves, and slip the beaded panel (C) into place. Attach bottom piece (D) to side pieces (B).

sit a spell
above right: Adirondack chairs offer comfort in a timeless design that suits any garden.

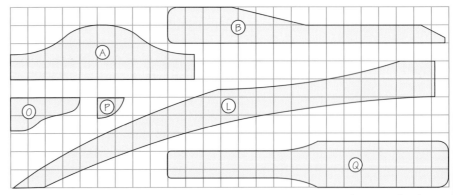

1 square = 2 inches

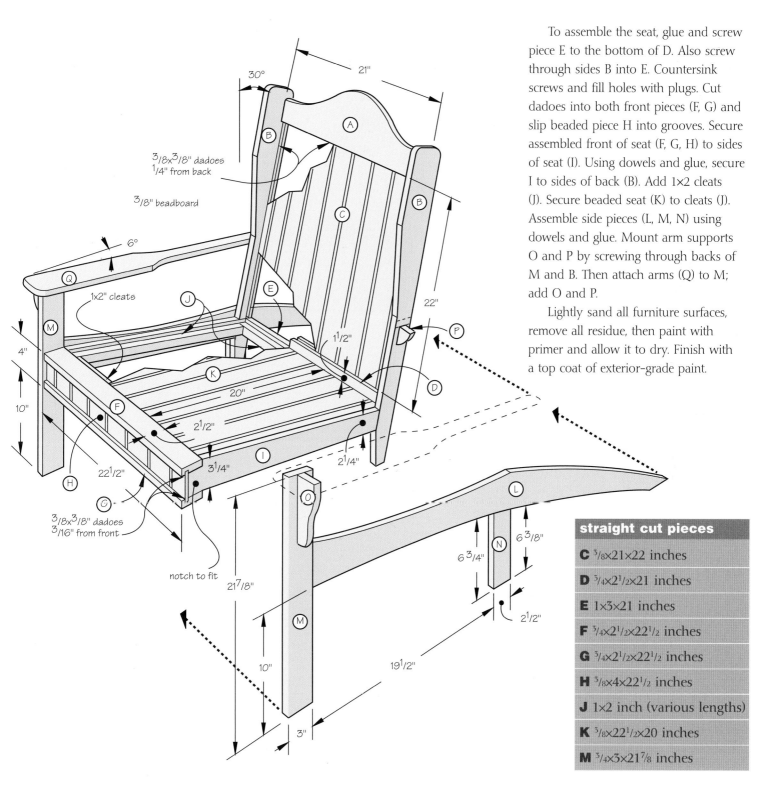

To assemble the seat, glue and screw piece E to the bottom of D. Also screw through sides B into E. Countersink screws and fill holes with plugs. Cut dadoes into both front pieces (F, G) and slip beaded piece H into grooves. Secure assembled front of seat (F, G, H) to sides of seat (I). Using dowels and glue, secure I to sides of back (B). Add 1×2 cleats (J). Secure beaded seat (K) to cleats (J). Assemble side pieces (L, M, N) using dowels and glue. Mount arm supports O and P by screwing through backs of M and B. Then attach arms (Q) to M; add O and P.

Lightly sand all furniture surfaces, remove all residue, then paint with primer and allow it to dry. Finish with a top coat of exterior-grade paint.

Diagram labels:

30°
21"
³/₈x³/₈" dadoes ¹/₄" from back
³/₈" beadboard
6°
22"
1×2" cleats
1¹/₂"
4"
10"
20"
2¹/₂"
22¹/₂"
3¹/₄"
2¹/₄"
³/₈x³/₈" dadoes ³/₁₆" from front
notch to fit
21⁷/₈"
10"
3"
19¹/₂"
6³/₄"
6³/₈"
2¹/₂"

straight cut pieces
C ³/₈×21×22 inches
D ³/₄×2¹/₂×21 inches
E 1×3×21 inches
F ³/₄×2¹/₂×22¹/₂ inches
G ³/₄×2¹/₂×22¹/₂ inches
H ³/₈×4×22¹/₂ inches
J 1×2 inch (various lengths)
K ³/₈×22¹/₂×20 inches
M ³/₄×3×21⁷/₈ inches

stacking-tray table

cost	make it	skill
$	weekend	advanced

you will need

- one 4×8-foot sheet of ⅜-inch beadboard (wainscoting)
- 1½×1½-inch pine stock (11 feet)
- ¾-inch pine stock (16 feet)
- ⅜-inch pine (18 inches)
- table saw with dado blades, or circular saw
- table router with ⅜-inch straight bit
- jigsaw
- cordless drill
- bit for no. 8 screws
- ⅜-inch bit for plugs
- exterior-grade wood glue
- 2-inch flathead phillips screws
- eight ⅜×1½-inch wooden dowels
- exterior-grade primer and paint

totable style

Use a table saw to cut all the pieces. Join the pieces with weatherproof glue; countersink screws. Cover screws with plugs. Rough-cut handle pieces (G), and use a jigsaw to make the radius cuts and handle cutouts. Cut a ⅜×⅜-inch dado into all tray sides (G, H, J). Attach handle pieces (G) to side (H). Slide in beadboard (I), and attach side (J) between handles (G). Glue on pads (K). Use stock lumber and ⅜-inch beadboard panels to construct the table. Cut a ⅜×⅜-inch dado into pieces B, C, and E. From the tabletop, cut ⅜×⅜-inch notches out of each corner to fit table legs (A, F). Assemble table by joining legs (A) to piece B, then attach side pieces (C) to legs (A). Slide beaded panel (D) into grooves, and secure E to legs (F), then legs (F) to (C) pieces. Finish the table and trays with primer; paint as desired.

fanciful colors

above right: **A stacking-tray table has eye-pleasing appeal. Paint the trays in colors that suit your fancy and your garden.**

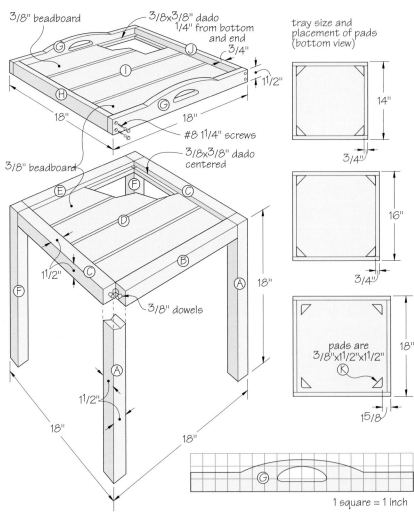

1 square = 1 inch

stowaway storage

right: This table is also a footrest that provides hidden storage. Use the compartment for stowing outdoor toys, or plastic serving ware and linens, or reading material, for days when you kick back and relax and nights when you entertain under the stars.

cost	make it	skill
$	weekend	advanced

multitasking table

Join the pieces with wood glue; countersink screws. Hide screw heads with plugs. Add a bit of glue to all grooves before sliding panels into place.

Use a table saw to cut the pieces for the footrest. Rough-cut the side-detail pieces (H, O); using a jigsaw, make the radius cut. Cut a ⅜×¼-inch dado in top and bottom rails (B, D, E, H, I, L, M, O), as well as in legs (A, F, J). Cut a ¼×⅜-inch rabbet in top frame pieces (P).

Assemble the base first, joining legs (A) to bottom rail (B). Slide beaded panel (C) into place. Join top rail (D) to legs (A). Attach bottom rail (E) between legs (A, F). Slide in panel G. Attach top rail (H). Follow the same process for the bottom with remaining pieces.

Join frame pieces (P) for the lid. Use wood glue and brads to secure panel (Q). Glue and nail ½-inch plywood bottom (R) to bottom rails (B, E, I, M). Attach the lid to the base with hinges.

you will need

one 4×8-foot sheet of ⅜-inch beadboard (wainscoting)

1½×1½-inch pine lumber (5 feet total)

1×6 (3 feet total)

table saw with dado blades

router with ⅜-inch straight bit

jigsaw

cordless drill

bit for no. 8 screws

⅜-inch bit for plugs

exterior-grade wood glue

⅜-inch flathead taper plugs

2-inch flathead phillips screws

2 hinges and screws

exterior-grade primer and paint

two hinges

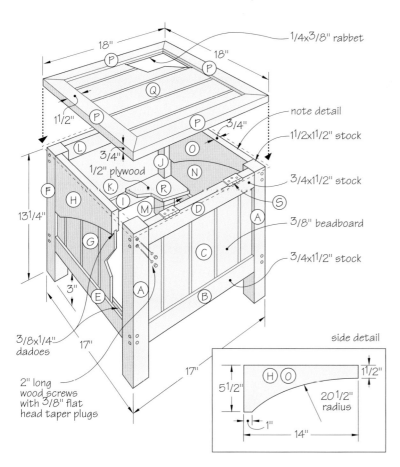

18"   18"   1/4x3/8" rabbet

11/2"   3/4"   note detail

3/4"   11/2x11/2" stock

1/2" plywood   3/4x11/2" stock

131/4"   3/8" beadboard

3/4x11/2" stock

3/8x1/4" dadoes   17"

2" long wood screws with 3/8" flat head taper plugs

3"

17"

side detail

51/2"   11/2"   201/2" radius

1"   14"

cost	make it	skill
$–$$	1 day	easy

you will need

two side supports: 4-inch-diameter, 6-foot-long branches

at least two crosspieces: 3-inch-diameter, 6-foot-long branches

additional flexible 6-foot-long branches

wood saw and pruning saw

pruner

carpenter's square

drywall nails

concrete bench

18-gauge wire

pliers

hammer

gloves

twist ties

bentwood beauty

Weave a little romance into your garden with a handmade bentwood trellis that makes a pretty and practical addition to a garden bench. Start by drawing the design on paper. The bent locust creation shown (*right*) resembles a chair back and is fitted to the bench, which uses recycled concrete curbing for the seat and salvaged architectural structures for the legs.

Harvest wood locally and bend it within a day or two of cutting, before it dries and becomes breakable. Support pieces should be at least 3 to 4 inches in diameter; the more decorative twigs should be as thick as your thumb.

bentwood-backed bench

right: **Combine a trellis and seating to create a nook with a one-of-a-kind look that doesn't require a large garden. Start with a seat that suits your garden's style; then adapt the directions for this bentwood-and-concrete scheme to suit your plans.**

1 frame Every trellis starts with a rectangle. Lay two crosspieces over two parallel uprights about 3 feet apart. Square every joint; use drywall nails to attach crosspieces to uprights. Nails will drive through the wood and protrude on the other side. To avoid driving nails into your work surface, slide a board beneath the trellis. Do not trim nails until both pieces are attached. Last, trim off the crosspiece that extends beyond the uprights.

2 reinforce Secure a 6-inch piece of 18-gauge wire around every joint for added strength. Using pliers, twist the wire over itself. Because wood shrinks as it dries, retighten wires after a month. Bend the two thin ends of the parallel pieces to form the top arch of the trellis. Overlap the branch ends using 6-inch lengths of wire to hold the arch in place. Secure the overlapped branches and reinforce the arch by twisting wire around the wood at 12-inch intervals.

3 bend Always check the flexibility of a branch before attaching it. Complete your design by attaching all remaining twigs. The general rule is to nail wood that's thicker than a pencil and to use wire when one piece of wood crosses another. As you add lattice shapes, Xs, hearts, or other decorative touches, step back often to keep perspective. Use twist ties to hold curves temporarily, or enlist the help of a friend.

yard & garden projects | **179**

swings

rockin' in the breeze

Who needs a porch if you hang a swing in your garden? Once you begin to swing and sway, you'll discover how a swing provides one of the best ways to relax after gardening.

As you plan your swingery, locate a level place that has good drainage for the support posts and provides a relaxing setting. Site the swing where there's a pleasant view and plenty of room to rock away the hours. Surrounding plantings should weave a tapestry that's a joy to see, but keep greenery at least 2 to 3 feet beyond the arc of the swing.

from ceiling to floor

Swings beckon strongest when summer peaks, and they generate a breeze with little effort. Cloak your swing with a robe of shade to provide optimum heat relief. A lath house, pergola, or lattice-top arbor will cast cooling shade over your swing, making a sought-after retreat for sizzling days.

Tuck blooming vines or climbing roses into soil near support posts to add a little floral drama. A plant canopy increases the degree of shade, and respiring greenery offers cooler temperatures. Include annual vines, such as morning glory and moonflower, to provide a dawn-to-dusk show. Trumpet vine, cardinal climber, grape, ivy, and akebia are other good vine choices.

cool swingers

right: **Instead of hanging a swing from a ready-made stand-alone frame, create a setting. Build a lath house or pergola to cultivate a sense of place and permanence, as well as shade for your garden.**

Below the swing, place a surface other than grass, especially if you have children. Foot-braking the swing wears away lawn with only a few slow-down drags. Flagstones or bricks offer firmer footing that's maintenance-free. Pea gravel and mulch require occasional raking and replenishing.

flowery decoration

left: Top your swing with a living canopy, such as this clematis. Train the vine to climb and twine along overhead supports.

outdoor cradle

left: A hammock bespeaks lazy summer days, often spent snoozing as the hammock gently rocks. String a hammock between two trees or suspend it on a ready-made stand. Hang a hammock when you plan to use it; otherwise, store it to protect the fibers from weather.

toolhouse

cost	make it	skill
$–$$	weekend	advanced

you will need

assorted redwood or cedar scraps

plywood scraps

sheet metal

½-inch wooden dowels

galvanized wood screws, various sizes

exterior-grade wood glue

tidy toolshed

A tiny shed keeps hand tools tidy and at the ready in a nearby garden spot. The shed shown is 17 inches tall, 15 inches wide, and 8 inches deep, but build your toolhouse with the dimensions that fit your needs. Materials for the project could be salvaged or bought new and distressed to appear rustic.

First construct the base; then build each component before assembling the house. The components include fencing, wall trellis, door and window, chimney, and interior hangers. Follow a glue and screw (or nail) pattern as you build. Glue parts together first; then add screws or nails. Assemble the house shell using plywood; then add wood siding. Next attach preconstructed components, including fencing and other details. Attach the shed squarely to the base; then screw plywood into place for a roof. Nail sheet metal in place last.

Place your toolshed in the garden, on a porch post or bench, or on an outdoor table. Display it where you'll be able to enjoy the fruits of your labor, as well as be able to grab tools for more work.

tool caddy

right: **A quaint toolhouse puts hand tools within reach for quick maintenance tasks. Gloves, trowels, plant markers, and other small helpers wait within.**

tool toting

Keeping tools handy is the key to efficiency in the garden. Options for corralling tools abound. If a cloth garden tote appeals to you, look for washable fabric, plenty of pockets, and a waterproof bottom. Baskets work well, but the tools easily become jumbled; be vigilant about removing unused tools. A 5-gallon bucket with a handle makes a nifty caddy. Pop a lid on it and the bucket becomes a seat for when you weed or take a breather in the garden.

set the stage

above: **The best gardens include workhorse features, such as a classic arbor and sturdy chairs, which combine form and function with decorative style. The toolhouse also fits that bill in this garden. Imagine this scene without the structures.**

potting house

a garden fantasy

A hodgepodge of old windows bound for the trash becomes a dream house for gardeners. The ultimate wizards of recycling, many gardeners specialize in taking what others consider castoffs and transforming them with creativity and elbow grease into treasures such as this enviable greenhouse (*right*).

A home-remodeling project and a similar structure displayed at a local garden show inspired the creation of this glass house. Follow this designer's lead. Instead of trashing replaced windows, compile them (or windows from a salvage store) into a light-filled retreat that's perfect for starting seeds, sipping lemonade, and puttering.

To get started, use our tips for creating your own garden getaway.

cover the bases

Site your house to face south, making the most of winter sunlight. If you live where mild winters rule, build a proverbial glass house using ground-to-gable glass, plexiglass, or plastic. In cold-winter locales, mount windows on a low wall to increase the structure's ability to retain heat. Glass or plexiglass are the best materials for a durable house in areas with strong or gusty winds.

Small spaces experience dramatic temperature swings. A greenhouse needs some type of ventilation to allow in fresh air and prevent the place from getting too hot and stuffy, which proves harmful to plants. Small, movable windows or vents near the top of the structure should suffice.

enhance the ambience

right: A garden house looks incomplete as a stand-alone structure. Surround it with plantings and decorative furnishings that complement its architectural style.

An 8×10-foot or 10×12-foot greenhouse provides ample space for starting seed flats and for storing frost-tender plants over winter, and it should not be hard to regulate its temperature. The climate of a larger greenhouse is easier to maintain than that of a smaller one.

simply charming

below: **Frame the house with a picket fence or a stone wall. Skirt structures with old-fashioned flowers, such as cosmos, hollyhock, peony, cleome, delphinium, and zinnia.**

glass-house alternatives

Easy-to-assemble greenhouse kits or prefabricated options make it simple to add a structure to your garden. Look for a size and style of greenhouse to suit the setting as well as your gardening skills. Also look for an energy-efficient model at an affordable price (including the cost of electricity and materials to operate it).

The advantages of having a greenhouse include getting a jump on growing in spring (start seedlings in a warm, covered area) and extending the growing season in fall (moving plants into the shelter). A greenhouse also enables you to grow a wider range of plants.

potting house

splendid salvage

Before building your glass garden house of
discarded windows, take inventory. Assess the
window sizes you have, then begin to piece them
together, as you would a puzzle. The structure
should be symmetrical. If necessary, trim windows
to fit the design. Strip the window frames. Sand
and paint them. Replace glazing that has cracked
or fallen out.

Establish a simple foundation for the house.
Concrete blocks work fine. Cover the blocks with
siding, bricks, or stonework, depending on your
garden's style. When positioning windows, suspend
frames from narrow strips of wood set inside
the house's timber framework. Caulk around the
windows to prevent leaks. This building method
makes replacing problem windows easier and is
also safer in earthquake-prone areas.

For flooring, consider that gravel lets water
drain into the ground below, whereas concrete
is easy to clean. Raise the entrance above ground
level for best drainage, and build a ramp leading
up to the door; lay a flagstone or concrete apron
just inside the doorway to make it easier to move
things in and out of the house. Make the house's
doorway and interior path wide enough to
accommodate a wheelbarrow.

In cold regions, heat the house to make it
habitable for plants during frosty periods. Provide
necessary electrical outlets and adequate space for
a heating system and a fan. Use rot-resistant wood
shelving or metal benches to hold plants.

garden plans

Locate your greenhouse where it provides a
substantial focal point. Traditionally placed in or
near a vegetable garden, a glass house should be
situated in a sheltered area away from shady tree
canopies, low frost pockets, and wind tunnels.

air exchange
above: Plexiglass
panels cut to size
form the angular
windows in the
gables of this
greenhouse. A system
of levers and handles
allows opening the
top windows from
ground level for
climate control.

embellished entry
right: A salvaged
door features a
bottom panel of
decorative trim.

Once your potting house is in place, arrange planting beds around it. Include blooming shrubs or dwarf fruit trees for old-fashioned charm. Add a patio outside the potting house to provide a place for relaxing between gardening chores. If shade is limited, create some with a trellis or latticework screen, to be covered with climbing roses, or add an umbrella and chairs.

task-oriented
left: Plan the interior of your potting house with its use in mind. Shelves and storage are vital for seed starting, as is a bin for holding soil. Hang tools in available vertical space. If you plan to overwinter garden equipment in the house, provide shelf space for that purpose. An interior water source, such as a spigot and garden hose, makes watering plants easier.

187

garden house

garden sheds

The ideal shed, whether fancy and furnished to the hilt or simple and strictly functional, contains a gardener's tools, togs, soil amendments, and pots. A shed stores and organizes garden gear in a location not too far from garden paths.

Situate a shed to be a focal point in your garden if you like. Design it with details that meld good looks and utility. Build windows, for instance, then add window boxes for a fanciful touch. Surround the shed with a porch that's wide enough to hold a pile of firewood as well as chairs and a table.

Soften the structure with climbing roses,

double-duty shed

right: **A 15×12-foot garden house boasts multiple personalities. During the day, this shed passes muster as a work space and utility building; after dusk, it segues into an entertaining mode as a serving center.**

clematis, or annual vines. Carve pathways that wander through your garden to the shed, making the journey as delightful as the destination.

Focus on function when furnishing the shed. If you plan to arrange bouquets of garden flowers there, rig a supply of running water. Add electrical outlets and lighting. Stock potting soil and birdseed in moisture- and critter-proof containers. Select a flooring material that's easy to sweep clean. Build doors wide enough to accommodate a wheelbarrow or a garden cart.

fresh-air flair
left: Latticework walls and an open, peaked roof give the shed an airy feel while containing the necessities for everyday garden chores. The utilitarian structure allows ample space for hanging tools on pegs.

garden house

open and shut

right: A waist-high counter tops storage shelves inside the garden shed. Drawers corral hand tools and flower-arranging supplies. Extra-long drawers accommodate long-legged plant markers and some tools.

plant caddy

below: A galvanized metal box keeps frequently used tools and other essentials neat looking and within easy reach. Ample, additional storage areas help minimize countertop clutter.

swanky shed

Supply your outbuilding with modern amenities. Beyond basic plumbing and electricity, you may wish to include a computer hookup to transform your shed into an office annex or studio. Run a phone line to it and eliminate mad dashes indoors to catch calls.

Where there's room, furnish a garden house to increase its uses. A refrigerator promises a convenient cold drink, and a wet bar earns its keep at garden parties. Include a dining table and chairs for cozy meals. Set up a desk or a drawing board and a stool; line a wall with a daybed.

basin beauty

left: **During garden parties, a soapstone sink keeps bottled beverages on ice in style. The sink also provides an ideal place to arrange flowers or scrub hands after gardening. A supply of clean towels waits in a nearby drawer.**

191

potting bench

work and play

For many gardeners, space-constrained yards and community landscape codes limit the addition of a full-scale potting shed. A multifunctional garden bench is an answer. Designed as a handsome piece of garden furniture, the unit combines a convenient place for potting with storage. As a serving surface, it makes entertaining easier.

Made from ½-inch plywood, the bench includes a place to inset plastic dishpans, which are perfect for holding soil, water, or drinks on ice. The roomy storage area accommodates pillows, linens, candles, and outdoor tableware.

neat and handy

right: **A well-designed potting bench reduces garden-gadget clutter. Store soil in a plastic garbage can; gather tools and plant labels in a decorative basket. Stack pots on a sliding shelf to enhance their access.**

out of sight

left: Storing outdoor cushions when not in use increases their longevity, but their bulkiness requires ample space. A tall sideboard-style addition to this potting bench protects pillows and other similar accessories. Stack lidded plastic bins inside the cupboard to increase storage efficiency.

potting bench inventory

A well-stocked potting bench is a putterer's paradise.

- Place bagged soil and amendments (sand, peat moss, perlite) in covered containers, such as plastic bins or garbage cans.

- Organize hand tools by function and size, using baskets or tall buckets. Separate sharp-bladed tools from digging tools to avoid accidental cuts.

- Run a length of hose from the nearest spigot to your bench; attach a turn-off valve. If you're plumbing from scratch, include a hot-water spigot.

- Gather the goods to sharpen, oil, and clean tools (lubricating oil, wire brush, sharpening stone, screwdrivers, pliers). Store them under cover.

cloches

cost	make it	skill
$	1 hour	easy

you will need

- 3- to 4-quart glass mixing bowl
- 18-gauge wire
- wire cutters
- pliers
- ½- to 1-inch-diameter wooden dowel, 4 inches long
- drill

spring fashion

Add an element of mystery and history to your garden by slipping seedlings under a classy glass cloche (pronounced kloshe), the French word for bell. Gardeners have used cloches for centuries to protect seedlings and lengthen the growing season.

Make a cloche from a clear glass mixing bowl. Use a bowl that is deeper than it is wide (an old standing-mixer bowl is perfect). If the bowl has a foot, as shown (*right*, at *right*), twist wire around the foot, leaving two loops opposite each other. Drill through a dowel from both ends, and insert a separate piece of wire through the wood to make a handle. Hook the wire to the opposing loops securely, as shown.

For a smooth-bottomed bowl (shown on *left* side of photo at *right*), cut four wires the depth of the bowl, plus 6 inches. Bend one end of each wire into a 2-inch-long hook. Slide the hooks over the bowl rim at four evenly spaced points. Position the remaining wire straight up the bowl sides, twisting the ends securely together at the top, making two loops of opposing wires. Add a handle.

homemade hothouse

right: **These old mixing-bowl cloches keep warm-weather crops, such as tomatoes, peppers, and eggplants, in cozy comfort as they get a jump on the growing season at least three weeks before the last average frost date.**

cloche encounters

A cloche acts as a portable hothouse that raises soil and air temperature around frost-tender seedlings. Placed over young plants in early spring and late fall, cloches extend the growing season by several weeks.

The trick to using them is to remember how cloches work. They protect seedlings by capturing and concentrating sunlight, much like a greenhouse. On bright days, it's key to vent the cloche by propping up one edge (or even removing the cloche entirely) to allow heat to escape. Otherwise, you might fry fragile foliage. Cloches also protect tender shoots from hungry rabbits.

season extenders
below: **A cloche acts like a suit of armor for seedlings, protecting young plants from the vagaries of spring and fall weather. Glass cloches last longer than plastic ones.**

bird places

flight of fancy

Befriend birds with all the amenities of a guest house: a fresh bath and a comfortable place to sleep or stay for a while. Blending function and beauty, birdhouses, birdbaths, and bird feeders represent some of the most favored garden embellishments.

splish, splash

Birds will come in droves to take baths and sing in your garden when you provide puddles aplenty. Use professional birdbaths, handmade hypertufa creations, or terra-cotta or plastic saucers. Keep baths full and clean; replace the water every two to three days. Scrub baths weekly with a solution of one part bleach to nine parts water to protect your winged friends from disease outbreaks. The sound of moving water attracts birds, so add a dripper or misting system to your bath. All you need is a water source to get dripping.

bathing beauties

above: In a natural-look garden, a hollowed-out rock provides a perfect place for birds to sip and splash. Locate birdbaths in the open but with sheltering shrubs and trees nearby so birds can fly to safety if threatened. Ground-level baths appeal more to birds than elevated ones, although birds frequent any water source that's regularly replenished.

sheltering tree

right: A towering birdhouse pole does double duty by acting as a prop for a stunning vine, such as this 'Comtesse de Bouchard' clematis. Position birdhouses in or near trees to provide cover for birds. If you plan to train vines up a birdhouse pole, plant vines when you set up the birdhouse to avoid disturbing nesting birds later.

birdy buffet

Although a diverse garden attracts birds with a variety of berries, seeds, and bugs, supplement the food selection year-round by setting out feeders and offering birds a varied diet.

As you plan your menu for the birds, choose feeders that accommodate the birds you want to beckon. Hang up a thistle feeder for finches, a nectar feeder for hummingbirds, and a roomy hopper filled with black-oil sunflower seeds for cardinals.

Look for feeders that blend function with durability and good looks. Beautiful blown-glass hummingbird feeders sparkle in the sunlight like jewels. Copper and cedar bird feeders add a lasting element of beauty to the garden. Supplement any seeds, fruits, or nuts you set out with a healthy garden brimming with bird-friendly plantings.

cozy inn

left: Add whimsy to your garden with a bird feeder that has all the charm of a country inn. Build a year-round magnet for birds with an enclosed platform-type feeder. For harsh-winter areas, make it a house instead, including only one small entrance hole. Place perches inside for roosting.

bird places

bird-friendly getaways

Hanging a birdhouse or two encourages birds to set up housekeeping in your garden. Select a house with decorative details, such as architectural gingerbread trim, bright colors, or fanciful painted designs, that will add eye-pleasing elements to the scene but make no difference to the birds. Be certain that the house you choose has been designed for outdoor use by birds. Houses present hazards to birds if they are painted inside, lack drainage holes, consist of materials that cause heat buildup, or have limited air circulation.

If you prefer to build a house, ensure the entrance opening is the proper size to admit only the bird types you desire. Use scrap or salvaged materials to create birdhouses with the charm of folk art, but without the price tag. Start with

bird b-and-b

right: **Combine housing and food in one location by attaching a platform feeding tray to a post and topping it with a birdhouse.**

victorian-style quarters

below: **Perch birdhouses on pedestals, porch posts, or other sturdy supports. If possible, face openings away from prevailing winds. Decorate posts with fanciful woodwork.**

a basic plan for a house, build it, then embellish it. Recycle sheet metal or cedar shingles for roofing, and extend the material over the entrance hole to protect birds in a downpour. Cut old shutter louvers to frame tiny windows; use leather strips for door hinges. Drill ventilation holes near the top back of the house, and attach the base or back with screws so the house can be opened for easy cleaning.

For information on birdhouse plans, contact your local county extension office, a garden center, or the National Audubon Society.

You can find more fun and doable garden projects at **www.bhg.com/bkgardenprojects**.

single-family housing
left: Because few birds will share housing space, equip your house with only one working entrance. Add other doors and windows for decorative purposes only.

in the round
far left: A birdhouse displays your building skills. Old moss-covered cedar-shake shingles find new life in this circular abode.

sturdy and stable
left: Give your birdhouse a firm foundation by mounting it on a wide, sturdy platform that attaches to a post at least 5 feet tall.

upright & alright

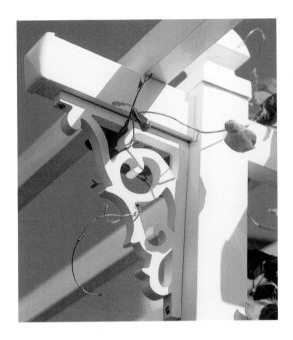

Plant supports give green things the backbone they often need to grow up.
think tall Trellises, tuteurs, obelisks, and similar structures tame rambling vines and climbing roses into neat towers of flowers and leaves. Best of all, they help conserve garden space and add vertical interest to the landscape.

Adopting reach-for-the-sky gardening techniques also removes tempting plants from the mouths of hungry rabbits.

Trellises and plant supports are among the easiest and most satisfying projects you can undertake. Most require minimal skills and can be completed in a day.

think again Look for ways to give new life to old items that have seen better days or scraps from previous projects that typically languish in the garage or the basement. Turn a rickety wooden ladder into an amusing plant tower. Top ordinary rerod with styrene balls for sturdy plant stakes with a touch of whimsy. Discover the ornate potential of a vintage metal bed frame by transforming it into a garden wall of sorts and hang a living wreath on it.

Use a tuteur or an obelisk as a purely decorative structure that makes an outstanding addition to the garden on its own, without a plant. Place a series of trellises side by side to achieve an artful screening effect (hiding an ugly chain link fence or blocking the neighbor's view of your outdoor dinner parties).

trellises

up, up, and away

Trellises take gardening to new heights without gobbling precious garden real estate. Start your vertical garden with annual climbers. It's as easy as pressing a few seeds into soil. Once vines climb the trellis, they'll continue reaching skyward. Annual climbers live life to the fullest in one growing season, flowering furiously until frost. All these high-rise beauties require is a steady support.

The type of support you provide depends on the plant. Twining vines (thunbergia, morning glory, hyacinth bean) wind along any straight support, such as latticework or bamboo poles. Tendriled climbers (cypress vine, cup-and-saucer vine, sweet pea) produce tiny stems that latch onto supports. They shin their way up best on mesh or strings. If you don't find the trellis you need here, visit **www.bhg.com/bkgardenprojects**.

luxury in bloom

right: **When choosing vines for trellises, consider if the plants will be viewed up close. 'Ville de Lyon' clematis *(shown)* shows off velvety blooms. Choose passionflower, cup-and-saucer vine, or akebia for their intricate blooms.**

copper beauty

right and *far right:* **Build a trellis from copper tubing and fittings cemented with weatherproof glue.**

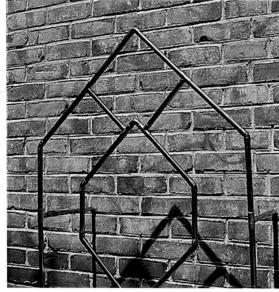

wall decor

left: **Accent posts with colorful trellises. When painting wooden latticework, apply a coat of exterior primer first; then add color with exterior latex.**

beautiful backdrop

below: **Lattice sections create visual screens as well as a home for vines or roses.**

Perennial vines, such as clematis, trumpet vine, ivy, cross vine, climbing hydrangea, akebia, and climbing snapdragon, ascend this way as well, so select their support systems accordingly. The prickles or thorns of climbing roses don't help the canes climb or cling to a support. Give Climbers and Ramblers ample support, lashing canes to the structure with loose ties.

anchor away

No matter what kind of trellis you select, secure it firmly in the ground. The weight of mature vines easily knocks trellises down in a windstorm. Anchor slender supports (such as bamboo structures, latticework, or copper trellises) by driving concrete reinforcing rods into the ground (either through or near the trellis); wire the trellis to the rods if possible.

trellises & roses

wall hangings

Take your roses and your garden to greater heights. Give Climbers, Ramblers, and other roses more than 4 feet tall the support they need to reach their potential by training them to a structure, such as an arbor, a pergola, or a trellis.

Structures add handsome and long-lasting architectural elements to the landscape. When embellished with roses, they become magnificent focal points. Train roses up a wall, along a roof, or into a tree. Guide them over entries, porches, and windows. Use the versatile nature of roses to soften hard angles and to hide eyesores, such as a dilapidated building or a compost pile.

cover up

right: '**American Pillar' (Rambler) scales a house with the assistance of trellis-work attached to the walls and roof.**

heavy-duty needs

above left: 'Dr. W. Van Fleet' (Climber) needs
a sturdy support, such as the corner of a house.
A delicate trellis wouldn't hold up under its
mature weight. This plant is guided by wires
anchored near the base of the plant and attached
to the soffit with eye screws.

modular means

above: Artful trellises, such as this modular set,
compose a pleasing view on a once-uninteresting
blank wall. One rose plant (in training) climbs the
supports without hiding them.

extra warmth

left: Fragrant, once-blooming 'May Queen'
(Rambler) tolerates cold but benefits from the
shelter and warmth provided by a stone wall.

trellises: wall trellis

cost	make it	skill
$$	1 day	moderate

you will need

two 2×4s
(23 inches long)

three 1×4s
(8 feet long)

2-inch #8 deck
screws

1¼-inch #8 deck
screws

½-inch roofing nails

exterior-grade
wood glue

30 feet of 14-gauge
solid bare copper
electrical wire

circular saw
or table saw

posthole digger

shovel

gravel

high-wire act

Cultivate living wallpaper by training a flowering vine up a trellis mounted against a wall. The result: a wall treatment that's lively as well as artistic, because the flowers attract bees and butterflies.

Use rot-resistant wood, such as cedar or pressure-treated pine, to give your trellis durability. Use exterior-grade stain or primer and paint to protect your trellis. Painting before you assemble pieces may spare you brushwork later.

Cut decorative grooves into the front faces of 1×4 posts using a table saw or circular saw with a rip guide. Cut a 2×4 to length for one of the upper caps and the lower cap; notch both with a jigsaw. Cut upper and lower rails from 1×4 stock, then rip the upper rail to 2½ inches wide.

pillar for plants
right: **A formal-looking trellis helps morning glories rise and shine, spreading their color across a drab wall.**

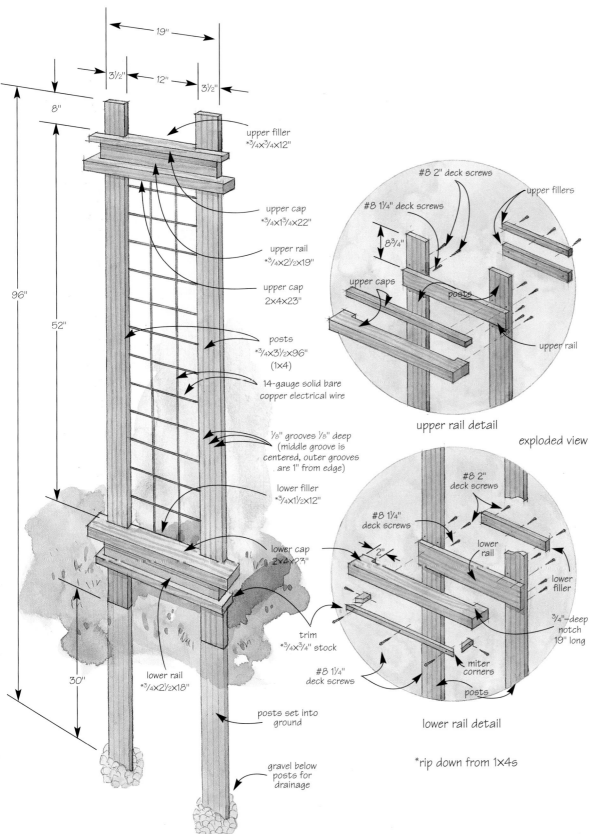

19"

3½" 12" 3½"

8"

upper filler
*¾x¾x12"

upper cap
*¾x1¾x22"

upper rail
*¾x2½x19"

upper cap
2x4x23"

96"

52"

posts
*¾x3½x96"
(1x4)

14-gauge solid bare
copper electrical wire

⅛" grooves ⅛" deep
(middle groove is
centered, outer grooves
are 1" from edge)

lower filler
*¾x1½x12"

lower cap
2x4x23"

trim
*¾x¾" stock

lower rail
*¾x2½x18"

posts set into
ground

30"

gravel below
posts for
drainage

#8 2" deck screws

#8 1¼" deck screws

8¾"

upper caps

posts

upper fillers

upper rail

upper rail detail

exploded view

#8 1¼"
deck screws

2"

#8 2"
deck screws

lower
rail

lower
filler

¾"-deep
notch
19" long

miter
corners

posts

#8 1¼"
deck screws

lower rail detail

*rip down from 1x4s

putting it together

Assemble posts, rails,
and caps as shown
(*left*). Fasten wood with
weatherproof glue and
deck screws (see
diagram for screw size),
driving screws from the
back side of the trellis.
Cut the ¾x1¾-inch
upper cap, and upper
and lower fillers,
and trim to size.
Glue and screw parts
into position.

Place the trellis
facedown. Partially
drive ½-inch roofing
nails around the
perimeter of the
opening every 4 inches.
Secure the wire end to
an upper rail nail; loop
the wire end twice
around the nail, then
wrap it around itself.
Take the wire to a nail
in the lower cap. Pull
the wire only taut
enough to straighten it.
Loop each vertical wire
once or twice around
each nail. Then repeat
the process for the
horizontal wires.

Dig 30-inch-deep
postholes and fill the
bottom with gravel.
Plumb the posts; backfill.

cost	make it	skill
$$	weekend	moderate

you will need

- two 2×2s (8 feet long) (A)

- twelve ³⁄₄×³⁄₄-inch lattice strips for crosspieces (B)

- twelve ³⁄₄×³⁄₄-inch lattice strips for uprights (C)

- twenty-four ³⁄₄×³⁄₄×1¹⁄₄-inch blocks (D)

- two 1×8s (8 feet long) for circles (E)

- exterior-grade wood glue

- hammer, power stapler

- 4d galvanized finishing nails

- carpenter's square

- galvanized staples or brads

- jigsaw

- exterior-grade primer, paint, and polyurethane

- two galvanized hinges, hardware

- two galvanized hooks, hardware

- handsaw or power saw

wall hanging
right: A handcrafted trellis looks good with or without vines.

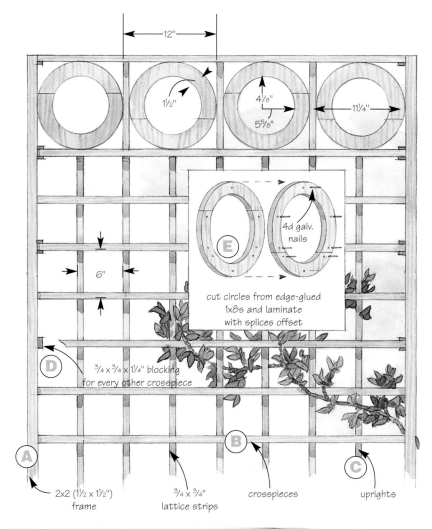

12"

1½"

4⅛"

5⅝"

11¼"

6"

cut circles from edge-glued
1x8s and laminate
with splices offset

E

4d galv.
nails

D

¾ x ¾ x 1¼" blocking
for every other crosspiece

B

C

A

2x2 (1½ x 1½")
frame

¾ x ¾"
lattice strips

crosspieces

uprights

builder's circle

For best results, choose materials of weather-resistant cedar, redwood, or pressure-treated pine. This trellis measures 6 feet high and 4 feet wide. Size your trellis to fit your site. The design works especially well to dress up a wall in a side yard or a courtyard. Train a vine on the trellis by positioning the structure over a planting bed or a container, such as a window box or an oblong planter.

Cut the frame stiles (A), lattice crosspieces (B), and uprights (C) to length, properly sizing openings for circles (E). Glue and nail support blocks (D) to stiles, spacing them 12 inches from center to center (see *left*). Lay out all the frame pieces on a flat surface and square them. Glue and nail or staple crosspieces (B) into place. Then attach uprights (C) to crosspieces, using the same method (glue and nail or staple).

Edge-glue the 1x8s together to create blanks for the circles. Cut them (when dry) into eight 11¼-inch-long pieces. Using a jigsaw, cut blanks into circles with a 5⅝-inch outside radius (4⅛-inch inside radius). Use exterior-grade weatherproof glue to laminate the circles, face-to-face, with the splices offset. Glue and nail the circles into position between the lattice strips at the top of the trellis.

finishing touches

Prime and paint the structure; then seal it using an exterior clear finish. Or leave a cedar trellis natural to weather gray. Mount the trellis to the wall with hooks at the top and hinges at the bottom, so it can be detached if the wall needs painting or cleaning.

round up support

left: An alternative design for skilled builders features a curved top and decorative posts.

trellises: fan trellis

cost	make it	skill
$$	2 days	advanced

you will need

³⁄₄×1¹⁄₂-inch lath:
six 84–inch–long
two 96–inch–long
one 12–inch–long
one 16–inch–long

4×4×84-inch posts

wood pieces:
³⁄₄×1¹⁄₂×16 inches
³⁄₄×1¹⁄₂×25 inches
³⁄₄×3¹⁄₂×12 inches
³⁄₄×3¹⁄₂×32 inches
³⁄₄×7¹⁄₄×25 inches
³⁄₄×10×24 inches
³⁄₄×⁵⁄₄×27 inches
⁵⁄₈×³⁄₄×³⁄₄ inches

1¹⁄₄-inch deck screws

2-inch deck screws

drill

screwdriver

circular saw

plant support

Build a classic-shape trellis of long-lasting cedar to highlight a spectacular rose. A series of trellises could form a backdrop for a garden, separate one area of a garden from another, or create privacy as well as attractive supports for plants. The trellis shown stands a foot away from the fence to allow air circulation around the plants. The trellises are held upright by 4×4 supports.

Cut all the pieces before assembling any of them. Build the trellis on a flat, level surface. If you plan to build a series of trellises, keep in mind that you don't need end posts for each one. Two trellises placed side by side, for example, would require three rather than four posts. Using 4×4s as posts, set two trellises at right angles to make a handsome corner and frame an area. Finish the structures using exterior paint or stain.

happy pair

right: **Clematis montana rubens and roses, such as bright red 'Dortmund' and white 'Alba', go together well with the trellises. Paired with the fence, they serve as a beautiful backdrop for a perennial garden.**

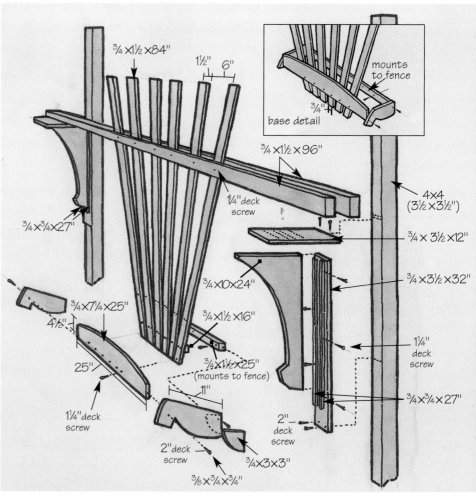

¾×1½×84"

1½" 6"

mounts to fence

¾" base detail

¾×1½×96"

4×4 (3½×3½")

¾×¾×27"

¼"deck screw

¾×3½×12"

¾×10×24"

¾×3½×32"

¾×7¼×25"

4½"

¾×1½×16"

¾×1½×25" (mounts to fence)

25"

1¼" deck screw

¾×¾×27"

11"

1¼"deck screw

2" deck screw

2"deck screw

¾×3×3"

⅜×¾×¾"

pretty support

left: A fan-shape trellis provides decorative support for a Climbing rose. Because the structure's design is an important part of the overall look, use roses that grow slowly, not rampantly, so they don't cover the trellis completely.

211

trellises: window frame trellis

cost	make it	skill
$–$$	afternoon	easy

you will need

old window or door frame

hammer

nails

1×2s (optional)

power drill/driver

wooden fence posts

tape measure

marker

3-inch drywall screws

screw eyes (size 112)

20-gauge galvanized wire

wire cutters

seeds for climbing annuals

window treatment

Forget curtains and sheers. Dress up an old window frame with draperies of annual vines. This window frame salutes the day with sun-worshipping morning glories. Cardinal climber, cup-and-saucer vine, thunbergia, and hyacinth bean provide similar eye-catching results.

This vintage window frame, salvaged from a church, provides height and substantive architectural trims for this one-of-a-kind trellis. You could also use a door frame or start from scratch by building a custom frame using new trim and molding. Consider where you will situate this trellis in your garden. Attach it to an existing fence or to wooden posts using drywall screws. Make this a garden decorating project for the whole family, from the construction to planting the seeds.

all dressed up

right: **A vintage window frame makes an upstanding garden feature or a screen. Multicolor morning glories eventually envelop the statuesque trellis.**

1 reinforce Move your window frame to a work surface that's level and accessible from all sides. If you use architectural salvage for the frame, consider reinforcing it. You don't want the structure to wobble when it's upright in the garden and exposed to wind. Brace the frame by nailing 1×2s over all the joints and possibly along the entire length of the back. This frame was three-sided to begin with; nailing a 1×4 across the bottom strengthened the structure.

2 measure Starting at the top of the frame and working down, measure and mark 6-inch increments along the inside edge of the frame. These are the points where you'll insert screw eyes. Do this on all four sides of the frame. Predrill pilot holes at each mark, then twist the screw eyes into place.

3 wire Position vertical wires first by looping wire through the first screw eye at the top left. Twist the wire to secure it, then pull it taut to the corresponding eye at the bottom. Add 10 inches to the wire's length; clip, then twist the excess length to secure it. Repeat the process until all vertical wires are in place. To create horizontal rows, start at one side and weave wire over and under vertical rows to the opposite eye. Secure the wire ends.

yard & garden projects | **213**

plant supports: willow tuteur

cost	make it	skill
$	2 hours	easy

you will need

8 willow posts, 7 to 8 feet long, 1½-inch diameter

25 feet of 14-gauge wire

metal macrame ring (or other type of ring), 18-inch diameter

50 thin willow rods, 5 to 6 feet long

eight 1-inch brown ring-shank panel nails

hammer

growing up

This twiggy tepee, known in garden design circles as a tuteur, arose from a French word meaning guide and instruct. In the garden, a tuteur guides and instructs climbing plants. But you don't have to speak French to make this classic design work for you. This willowy beauty uses tree trimmings, but windfall or prunings from locust, fruit, or cedar trees can also be used.

Begin by gathering eight willow posts. About 10 inches from the top of the posts, wrap 5 feet of wire around the bundle several times. Twist and snip the wire ends.

Have someone help with the next two steps. Space the posts evenly apart, forming a tepee. Insert the metal macrame ring inside the posts to about a third of the way up the form. Use wire to secure the ring in place temporarily. You'll remove the ring when you're done weaving, so don't snip the wire ends.

beyond the garden

right: **This twig-entwined tower blends the artistry of basket weaving with a casual approach to function. Once you master the weaving techniques, create tuteurs of all sizes to fit large outdoor containers or serve as small tabletop centerpieces.**

Trim eight willow rods to equal length. Nail the base of one rod to the inside of a post just above the metal ring. Weave the rod over and under the next two posts counterclockwise, leaving the end free. Nail another rod to the next post clockwise. Weave it over and under the next two posts counterclockwise, placing it just above the first rod. Leave the end free. Continue in this fashion until each post has a rod nailed to it. Repeat the weaving technique: One at a time, weave the rods over and under the next two posts counterclockwise, until all rods are woven. Weave eight more rods directly above this first section. No need for nails now; simply wedge rods between posts.

Repeat the process 20 inches above the weaving, using 16 more rods. Finish by twisting the willow rods to form a ropelike strand. Twine the willow rope around the tower until you reach the top. Tuck the ends into the wrapped-rod tops.

Conceal the top wire using a willow rod. Remove the metal ring spacer. Trim the post tops. Push the tower into the ground. Anchor it using a metal rod, if desired.

Plant towers provide a sense of height in the garden. Other height-inducing plant supports include an old wooden ladder or a lamppost.

rung by rung

above: Transform a rickety wooden ladder into an artful support for gregarious vines. Spin a little whimsy into the scene with a ladder-spanning spiderweb made from grapevine and attached to the uprights.

timeless decor

left: A tuteur, with traditional good looks, supports plants in style. Standing unadorned by greenery, the structure adds an outstanding visual element.

yard & garden projects | **215**

plant supports: vine poles

cost	make it	skill
$	1 day	moderate

tower of flowers

Planting a pole for climbing vines will reward you with a handsome column of colorful blooms.

Build the pole with weather-resistant wood. Cut 24-inch crossbars using 1×2s. Mark curved ends with a compass; cut ends with a band saw or jigsaw. Smooth the ends using sandpaper. Cut a 1×4 into spacers for the middle layer of the pole: one 9¼ inches long, five 8½ inches long, and one 35¼ inches long.

On a flat surface, position the 9¼-inch spacer flush with the top of a 1×4, aligning edges. Fasten pieces face-to-face with weatherproof glue and finishing nails. Place a crossbar against the bottom of the top spacer, centering it end to end. Glue and nail it into position. Repeat this process with remaining spacers and crossbars. Glue and nail the final 1×4 face-to-face to complete the pole.

Cut and sand the curve at the top of the vine pole. Drill a 1-inch-diameter hole through the curved top. Seal the pole using exterior paint or stain. Dig a 30-inch-deep posthole, adding 6 inches of gravel for drainage (see page 85). Have someone hold the post plumb as you backfill the hole.

blooming skyscraper

right: **Annual vines started from seed, such as thunbergia, or black-eyed Susan vine, grow up where space is at a premium.**

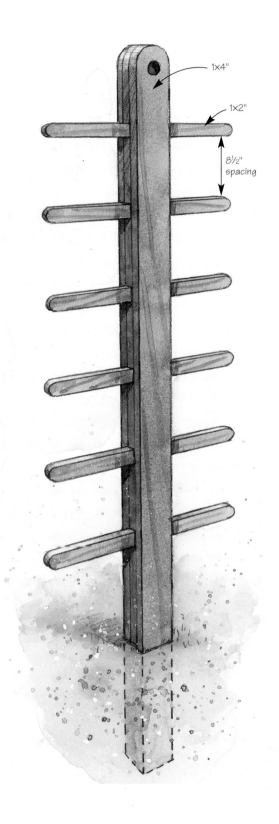

1×4"

1×2"

8½" spacing

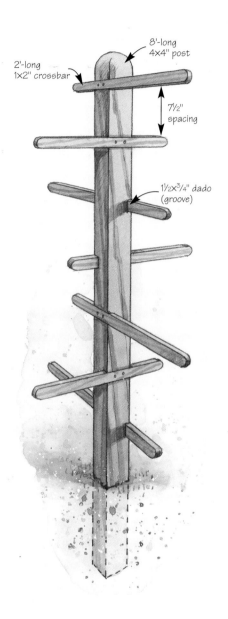

8'-long 4×4" post

2'-long 1×2" crossbar

7½" spacing

1½×¾" dado (groove)

signpost pole

Once annual vines break through soil, they reach for the sky. This alternative version of the vine pole features crosspieces poised on varying sides of a post and represents an easier building project. Mark vines' growth with imaginative signs painted on crosspieces of the pole, if you like. Involve the whole family in this project, inviting everyone to contribute their favorite locations (include distances from home to there) for a sign. Build the pole using an 8-foot-long 4×4 made from weather-resistant lumber with 1×2s as crossbars. Add names and mileage to the signs using acrylic paint; seal with a clear varnish.

great vines for climbing

bottle gourd	cypress vine	purple bell vine
canary creeper	hyacinth bean	spanish flag
climbing nasturtium	love-in-a-puff	sweet pea
climbing snapdragon	moonflower	thunbergia
cup-and-saucer vine	morning glory	variegated hops

plant supports: obelisk

cost	make it	skill
$	weekend	easy

you will need

four 2×2s
(5-feet long) (A)

14 feet of 1×2
slatting (B, C, D,
and E)

countersink drill bit

protractor

circular or table saw

heavy-duty
construction adhesive

twenty-four 2-inch
deck screws

power screwdriver
with no. 2
phillips bit

tape measure

scrap wood and
nails for tacking

fine-grit sandpaper

exterior-grade stain
or primer, paint,
and polyurethane

eye-full tower

An obelisk forms a captivating pyramid that's every bit as fanciful as it is functional. Left unclothed with vines, this pointed structure serves as garden sculpture. Dressed in climbing bloomers, an obelisk becomes a supporting actor, holding aloft a bower of flowers. For vines with stems that wind upward (morning glories, beans, and thunbergia), push seeds into soil around the base of the obelisk. Press your pillar into service as a plant support for tendriled vines (peas, cardinal climber, and cup-and-saucer vine) by tacking fishing line onto bottom slats and peaks.

Build similar tepee-type structures from thick bamboo canes lashed together at the top with twine or topped with a decorative finial.

get the point

right: **An obelisk adds a structurally classic look in the garden, providing a place for vines to twine or serving as a focal point. Skirt your pointed tower with perennial bloomers that soar to various heights, such as these yellow coreopsis and pink bee balm.**

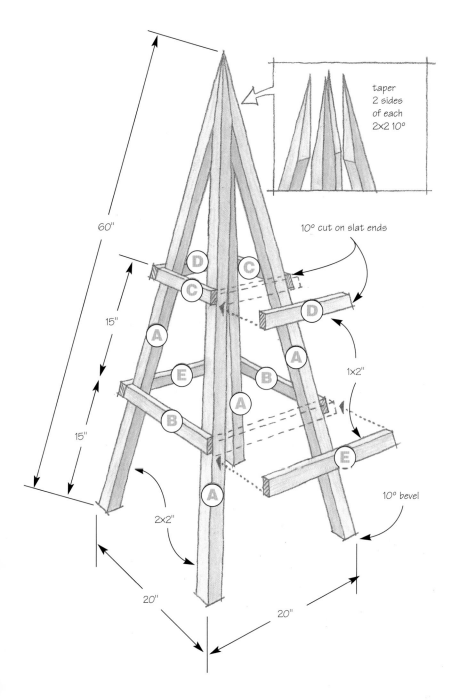

taper
2 sides
of each
2x2 10°

60"

10° cut on slat ends

D   C
  C

15"

A   D

E   A

B   A

15"   1x2"

B

2x2"   E

A   10° bevel

20"

20"

aspire higher

Simple enough for novice woodworkers, this obelisk assembles easily in a day. Add another day to allow the wood finish to dry.

Start with rot-resistant wood such as cedar. Predrill screw holes using a countersink drill to prevent splitting the wood. Mark 10-degree angles (on two sides) from a corner of the top of each leg (A) using the protractor. Make cuts. Lay two legs on a flat surface, apply adhesive, and press the pointed ends together. Screw tips together by driving one screw from the left through the joint and the other from the right through the joint. Glue and screw the two remaining legs in the same manner.

Measure and mark 15 and 30 inches up from the bottom of the legs. Temporarily tack the legs together at the proper spread using a piece of scrap wood. Make pieces B and C by placing a 1x2 just below the marks on the legs. Mark cut lines on each 1x2 using the outsides of the legs as guides. Cut pieces to size and attach using adhesive, followed by one screw per joint. Then set both pairs of legs upright and screw them together at the top. Measure to make sure the spaces between legs are equidistant. Make pieces D and E by holding a piece of 1x2 against the legs. Use brace ends (B and C) to mark where cuts will be made. Assemble as shown using weatherproof glue and screws. Bevel the leg ends so the obelisk can sit flush on the ground. Alternatively, bury the ends in soil until the obelisk is level. Smooth rough edges using sandpaper.

For a natural, weathered look (gray cedar), apply wood preservative or wood-tone stain. If you prefer to paint the obelisk, apply exterior-grade primer first, followed by a coat of exterior-grade latex. After it's dry, tuck your obelisk into a garden bed and admire your handiwork.

plant supports: stake toppers

cost	make it	skill
$	1 hour	easy

you will need

- plant stakes
- toppers
- power drill (optional)
- screws
- paint (optional)
- exterior-grade weatherproof glue

high stakes

Transform your garden into a gallery of stake sculpture by topping your favorite stem supports with life's flotsam and jetsam (most often found in junk drawers, craft closets, and workshops). Enjoy playing matchmaker by fitting doodads to stakes. If you choose objects that might hold water, drill holes in their bottoms so rain can drain. Attach toppers to stakes using screws or weatherproof glue. Allow glue to dry overnight before setting stakes in the garden. Paint stakes or toppers, if desired, using bright exterior colors.

ramrod straight

right and *below:* **Decorative stake toppers, which reduce the hazard of sharp stakes standing unseen among leaves and stems, offer protection from an eye poke.**

stake toppers

1. wooden beads on bamboo
2. plastic foam ball and fishing bobber on rerod
3. bouncy rubber ball on metal pole
4. cork, copper wire, and beads on plastic pole
5. plastic foam ball on rerod

stick 'em up!

above: A variety of stake toppers—a terra-cotta pot, wooden beads, copper wire and beads in a cork, a drawer pull, a watering can refrigerator magnet, a painted wooden pinwheel, and a plastic ornament—reach for the sky. Stakes include copper pipe, a closet rod, a broom handle, and plastic-coated steel.

pretty props

left: Almost anything can become a stake topper. A brass doorknob, a wooden finial, a pot of violas, a glass doorknob, and a large glass marble fit atop a variety of supports, such as bamboo and rerod.

wreath on trellis

cost	make it	skill
$–$$	1 hour	easy

you will need

plants in cell packs
or 2-inch pots

cupped wire
wreath form

sphagnum moss

soilless potting mix

slow-release fertilizer

floral wire or
fishing line

floral pins

scissors

disposable gloves

garbage-can lid

ring around posies

Deck your garden
with living wreaths.
This circle of life dresses
up the garden, hanging
on an iron bed frame
that transforms easily
into a trellis. Hang
wreaths in partial
shade; water as needed.

go for the gold
right: This wreath
features a golden
theme: yellow violas,
'Goldchild' ivy,
'Golden Fleece'
Dahlberg daisy,
and golden sage.

1 gather materials Purchase a cupped wire wreath form at a crafts or hobby store. Choose plants in 2-inch pots or cell packs. Plants that thrive in wreaths include viola, alyssum, ivy, alpine strawberry, and small-leaf groundcovers. Select creeping or vining plants or ones with petite flowers. Herbs such as trailing rosemary, thyme, and marjoram also make pretty wreaths.

2 prepare the bed Soak sphagnum moss in water until saturated. Then squeeze out excess water. (Wear disposable gloves when handling moss.) Line the concave side of the wreath form with moss; fill with a mound of soilless potting mix. If the mix doesn't contain a slow-release fertilizer, add it at the recommended rate.

3 add plants Pop plants out of their nursery pots, position them on the potting mix, then tuck the root balls into the mix. Fill in between plants with added potting mix and moist moss. Secure the moss with floral pins. Wrap the wreath with floral wire or fishing line, gently working your way between the plants and around the wreath.

4 care Water the wreath thoroughly by soaking it in a garbage-can lid full of water. Then hang the wreath using stout hardware. Check the wreath daily; take it down and soak it when it feels dry.

yard & garden projects | **223**

home for a plant

Containers play various roles in a landscape. Use them as focal points in the garden. Employ a large, empty urn as a piece of art, on its own or grouped with other pots. Express your personality and greet visitors by decorating your home's entryway with a potted garden. Combine plants with intriguing colors and textures in a single, large container that boasts huge impact.

movable feast The only dilemma you may face when selecting a pot for your garden is choosing from the many materials and finishes available. Consider classic concrete and natural terra-cotta (and lightweight look-alikes for both) as well as rustic wood and contemporary self-watering planters. Synthetic pots last longer and tolerate freezing winters better than most other lightweight materials. They're also easier to move around.

one of a kind The most enticing aspect of gardening in containers is the freedom it gives you to experiment and have fun. Grow tender plants that you've always wanted but couldn't grow in your region's climate; carry them indoors, pot and all, to live over winter. Count on containers to fill gaps in the garden: Pot spring- and summer-flowering bulbs; plant perennial and tropical bloomers with annuals for all-season color.

Change your window-box plantings from season to season for eye-catching appeal. If you're tired of looking at plain terra-cotta pots, give them a facelift with a little paint. Imagine all the potential homes for plants, from a wooden crate or a decrepit wagon to a worn basket or rusted washtub.

containers

portable gardens

Oh, the places they'll go! Containers make gardening
so accessible, easy, and variable that they have
virtually no drawbacks. Pots let you garden in
otherwise impossible places and enliven any
setting with their colorful plantings. Set pots in a
window box and attach it to a sill or a deck
railing. Set a planter on each tread of an entry
stairway. Suspend baskets from eaves, overhead
beams, and pergolas. Wherever you find a bit of
empty space, you have a spot for a container.

The ability to change or rearrange pots and the
plants in them in a matter of minutes makes this
kind of gardening fun. Just follow a few simple
guidelines: Combine plants with similar moisture
and light requirements, water them frequently
during the hottest days of the year, and pay
attention to the cold tolerance (or tenderness)
of the plants you choose.

unlimited choices
right: From small
3-inch plastic pots and
petite ceramic urns to
large 5- and 10-gallon
terra-cotta planters
and strawberry jars,
the range of sizes and
materials available
today extends the
scope of gardening in
containers. Choose a
spot for a garden and
you'll find a container
to match it.

personal expression

left: Turn an eyesore into an asset using a container. In this case, an old brick pillar becomes a useful pedestal for an outstanding potted rose. Depending on the plants and pots you choose, container gardens also become an expression of your personality. Go formal or informal. Indulge a passion, such as growing herbs. Create the water garden of your dreams without all the work.

high flight

below left: Use trailing plants for their architectural characteristics as well as their bright flowers or foliage. Choose traditional trailers, including petunias and ivy geraniums, or unusual ones, such as these succulents. Hang them where they'll receive adequate light while creating a dramatic effect.

potted advantages

Compared with in-ground plantings, potted gardens are more temporary, but they also reward spontaneous design and a willingness to change them. Experiment freely with new plants and combinations, knowing you can easily redesign the planters next season. Avoid the chore of amending garden soil, whether it's infertile or drains poorly. Overcome shady locations and brighten dark corners with pots of colorful flowers. Extend the growing season by moving plants indoors over winter. Grow plants you otherwise would not include in your garden. Use limited space more efficiently or break up large areas in your landscape with pots. Keep invasive plants contained so they don't overrun your garden.

containers

pot luck

Container gardens come to life in all sorts of shapes and forms, but the result remains the same: instant gratification. Pleasure abounds in a pot of colorful flowers that's easily planted and tended. Think of containers as accessories for the garden. Use them to personalize the scene, provide room for portable plantings, and allow you to grow plants you might not include in permanent planting areas.

Pressing vintage housewares and old garden gear into service as pots is fun and easy. Look for containers with character and room for roots to grow, such as an upended metal mailbox, a willow

a tisket, a tasket

right: **No need to throw away worn baskets. Line them with porous landscape fabric, fill with soil, and plunk in plants.**

cracked pots

below: **Broken bits of pottery and glass transform an ordinary container into a work of art. See page 165 for how-to information.**

laundry basket, or a rusted watering can. Plant in anything that will hold soil, from old drawers to a leaky teakettle.

For containers made of cane, wicker, or metal mesh, line the interior with wet sphagnum moss, plastic garbage bags, porous landscape fabric, or an empty soil bag. Remember to poke a few drainage holes in the bottom. When filling wooden containers, seal the wood first (especially seams and corners) with several coats of a waterproof finish before adding soil.

All containers need drainage, so drill holes if necessary. If you prefer to keep the container intact, use it as a cachepot (that's French for "put the plants in a cheap green plastic pot that fits inside the fun container").

Use a lightweight soilless potting mix developed for container gardening. Mix organic or pelletized slow-release fertilizer and water-holding crystals into soil before planting. Water plants whenever the soil feels dry.

For more tips and advice on container gardens, visit **www.bhg.com/bkcontainergardens**.

lush locks
above left: **Every day's a good-hair day when tangles of blooms form the tresses. This witty 'do unfurls in 'Elijah Blue' fescue accented with a tiara of daisies.**

seedy dreams
left: **A vintage seeder sees new life as a planter. Use antique pieces only if you don't mind hastening their deterioration outdoors.**

yard & garden projects | **229**

wagons

potted pleasures

Consider container plantings a stylistic part of your garden's decor. Match them to suit your mood, to highlight plants in their prime, and to transform an otherwise bare and boring area of the garden into a spot of color.

The mobility of potted plants gives them an advantage over earthbound plantings. A wheelbarrow, wagon, or dolly makes it easy to move pots, whether you want a colorful display near an entry, in the shade, or in the limelight at an outdoor party. Master the tricks to create gatherings that delight the eye.

choose a focal point Use an old wagon or wheelbarrow to make a collection of pots a focal point in the garden. Change the plants in the display as you desire. Protect surfaces; use pot saucers or pot feet under containers to prevent water from pooling.

combine container shapes Mix bowl-shape pots with ones that are tall and trim, broad or long. Set low pots in front, near the edges of container displays. Set taller pots in the back.

move them up Raise containers on pot feet, pedestals, plant stands, inverted pots, or bricks. Stabilize elevated containers to prevent them from toppling on windy days.

wagons ho

right: **Round up pots overflowing with pretty foliage and flowers into an antique wagon for a plant display that can easily be changed.**

roll 'em

left: Press an old wheelbarrow into service as a container caddy, loading it with pots of flowers. Surround it with planters made from found objects, including well-worn shoes.

portable color

below left: A collection of geraniums seems to bloom brighter inside a blue wagon.

focal point

below: Use a wagon to elevate a container and add strong interest to an otherwise drab group of small pots.

in the garden

defining art

Large or small, any garden benefits from potted
plantings. Placed strategically, large containers
create strong focal points. As architectural elements,
they instantly add structure and form. Combining
a simple four-legged obelisk and twining clematis
with a square planter, for instance, makes a
handsome, living sculpture.

Use rows of pots to define the perimeter
of a garden bed, to form a wall to screen an
unattractive view, or to mark steps in the garden.
Brighten a shady spot under trees with containers
of light-color plants. Place containers in the garden
as permanent features or temporary ones. When
lightweight enough to be movable, a large pot of
colorful blooms creates drama and intrigue.

functional forms

above and *right:* Planters with obelisks add
structure and height to the garden while helping
to define planting areas as well as pathways. The
large, empty amphora in the center of the
bisecting paths anchors the design. The potted
evergreen stands at left in the garden.

obelisk in a container

cost	make it	skill
$	weekend	moderate

you will need

2×2s: four
5–6-foot lengths of
cedar or redwood;
one 2×2-inch
cube for core

decorative finial

2-inch deck screws

circular saw

wood stain or
exterior latex paint
(optional)

drill with ¼-inch bit

galvanized fence
staples or screw
eyes (optional)

nylon wire or
string (optional)

build an obelisk

Add vertical interest to a garden with supports such as tepees, obelisks, and trellises. These structures provide extra growing space for even the smallest garden. Adapt the height of the uprights (or legs) to suit the size of the containers. Use three- or four-legged tepees to support your climbing plants.

Obelisks look as good unadorned as they do with plants twining their way up and around the legs. Trellises made with lumber, lattice, or netting supply toeholds for plants.

great plants for climbing and vining

black-eyed susan vine	madeira vine
canary vine	mandevilla
carolina jessamine	moonflower
clematis	morning glory
climbing rose	nasturtium
honeysuckle	passionflower
ivy	sweet pea
jasmine	trumpet vine

lend a hand

right: Assist vines, such as this Jackman clematis, in climbing an obelisk by crisscrossing nylon twine up the legs. Use screw eyes to hold the twine in place.

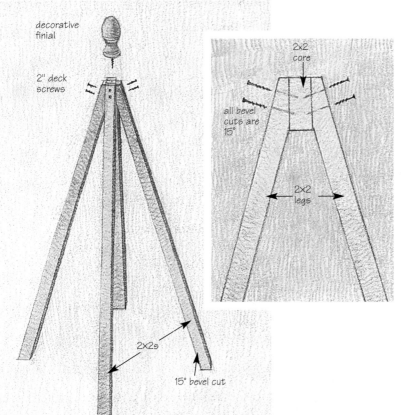

decorative finial

2" deck screws

2x2 core

all bevel cuts are 15°

2x2 legs

2x2s

15° bevel cut

showing off

above: One advantage of pairing clematis with an obelisk is that its twining stems usually do not completely cover the support. The structure, whether obelisk or trellis, remains an important part of the planting's overall design.

details, details

Vary the height of this easy-to-build obelisk from 5 to 6 feet tall. Make the height of the finished structure in scale with the size of your planter. Predrill starter holes in the top and sides of a 2×2 cube. Cut each top and bottom of the 2×2 legs at a 15-degree angle; join the top ends by attaching them to the sides of the cube using deck screws. Screw the finial into the top of the cube. Paint or seal the lumber before assembling, or leave it unfinished to weather naturally. Insert the obelisk legs at least 4 to 6 inches deep in the soil-filled planter.

window boxes

cost	make it	skill
$	1–2 hours	easy

you will need

window box: size to match your window ledge; at least 4 inches deep, with holes for drainage

lightweight potting mix or soilless mix

plants in 3–inch pots

eye-level beauty

Nothing dresses up a house, from an indoor point of view as well as outside from the street, like window boxes resting on sills or hanging just below. The only tricky part to gardening in window boxes is reaching them to remove spent flowers and to water, but a watering wand attached to a hose helps with the latter chore.

Window gardens span the seasons. To make changes easier, use plants in their pots instead of putting them directly in soil in the box. When using plants already in pots, you can replace spring–blooming bulbs with summer–flowering annuals, followed by low-growing evergreens, such as juniper, for winter color.

adaptable plants

right and *below:* This English-style planting does well in full or partial sun, although the geraniums and periwinkles flower best in exposures with at least six hours of sun daily. If the petunias become too leggy by midsummer, trim them back hard by one-third.

plants

1 petunia

2 madagascar periwinkle

3 ivy

4 geranium

5 lobelia

1 design Select plants with a variety of growth habits—upright, bushy, and trailing—and with complementary or matching colors. Remember to consider the shapes and colors of foliage as well. Fill the window box three-fourths full with a good potting mix. Stir in water-retentive crystals and a slow-release fertilizer to cut down on watering and feeding during the season; follow label directions. Setting the window box in place before planting makes the job easier.

2 plant Set the plants in their pots on top of the soil; rearrange them until you like the design. Place taller plants toward the back and either the center or the ends. Fill in spaces with bushy plants. Put trailing plants in front to drape over the edge. Use vining plants, such as dwarf morning glory, on the ends; attach small trellises to the box or to the window frame for them to climb on. Unpot plants and set them in the soil at the same depth they were growing before.

3 maintain Water thoroughly after planting. Check soil daily and water to a depth of about 2 to 3 inches when it is dry. To keep the garden neat, pinch off or deadhead spent blooms and remove yellowed or dead leaves. Fertilize monthly if you didn't mix a slow-release fertilizer in with the soil. In midsummer, cut back (by one-third) straggly or nonflowering plants, such as pansies and sweet alyssum, to promote reblooming through the cooler days of autumn.

yard & garden projects | **237**

wooden boxes

cost	make it	skill
$–$$	1–2 days	moderate

you will need

- ¾-inch plywood exterior-grade (box)
- 2×2s (posts)
- 1×2s (trim and cap)
- four 2-inch wooden ball finials
- galvanized screws or nails
- drill with ¾-inch bit
- circular saw

classic style

A simple wooden cube forms the basis for many different planter styles. Add posts and finials for a classic look. Attach a trellis to a 6-foot-long plain box to create a decorative privacy screen next to the patio. Turn old crates and baskets into containers for edibles in a matter of minutes. The possibilities are limited only by your imagination and, in some cases, by your do-it-yourself skills. When building wooden containers, start with cedar or another weather-resistant lumber. Always make drainage holes in any wooden container.

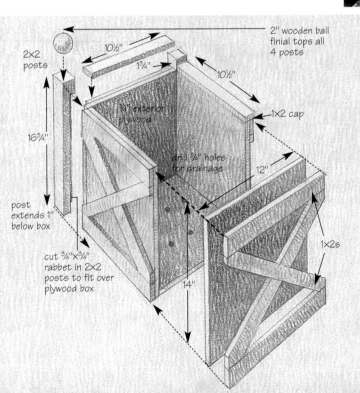

2×2 posts

10½"

1¾"

10½"

2" wooden ball finial tops all 4 posts

¾" exterior plywood

1×2 cap

16¾"

drill ¾" holes for drainage

12"

post extends 1" below box

cut ¾"×¾" rabbet in 2×2 posts to fit over plywood box

14"

1×2s

[handwritten: PRIVACY PLANTER]

greens envy
above left: Plant a garden of lettuces and greens in wooden crates that started life with a different purpose: holding bulbs, strawberries, and other fruits, such as peaches.

country accent
above: The simplicity of pansies pairs beautifully with the casual look of wood. Mix flower colors for a lovely display.

privacy planter
left: Attach a lattice screen to the back of a planter. It will provide privacy as well as a handsome support for climbing plants, if desired.

shallow bowl

cost	make it	skill
$	1 hour	easy

you will need

- wide, shallow terra–cotta container
- soilless potting mix made of peat moss and vermiculite
- piece of window screening
- assorted perennials, ornamental vegetables

temporary color

No matter what the season, containers bursting with color help to brighten dull spots, accent a patio or deck, or highlight your favorite flowers. All it takes is a bit of advance planning. By observing when certain plants peak in performance and acknowledging when they have passed their prime, you will recognize when it's time to remove them from the container and replace them. If they are perennials, resettle them in a garden bed.

When you go to the garden center, visualize how the plants will look together, even if you don't have the container with you. Lay out your design ideas in your shopping basket or wagon.

color now

right and *below:* **Start with mature plants to create containers with immediate impact. For longer bloom time, of course, select younger plants.**

plants

1 *aster novi-belgii* 'crimson brocade'

2 chrysanthemum

3 sedum

4 variegated ivy

5 korean rock fern

6 ornamental cabbage

1 select a pot Wide, shallow containers make attractive homes for an abundance of plants. Starting with mature plants means this is a temporary planting, and you don't need to be concerned about the long-term fertility of the soil. A lightweight, soilless mix of peat moss and vermiculite provides an adequate support for the plants. If you prefer, use garden soil or a packaged potting mix. Before adding the mix, place a piece of window screening over the drainage holes to keep them from clogging.

2 pack them in For an instant show of color, set plants close together. Pay attention to colors and textures; they should complement one another. Set a plant with frilly leaves next to one with very fine leaves. Offset those with bolder leaves, such as chrysanthemums, and those with lighter green foliage, such as sedums.

Scoop a depression in the mix and set the plants in at the same depth as they were growing in their nursery pots. Water the finished planting well. Keep the soil mix evenly moist.

yard & garden projects | **241**

tire planter

cost	make it	skill
$	2–3 hours	moderate

you will need

- automobile tire with rim attached
- chalk
- finely serrated, sharp knife
- work gloves
- tin snips or pruner
- latex paint and paintbrush
- potting mix
- plants, as desired

recycled art

The idea of using a tire as a planter is decades old, but the design here gives it a new spin and turns it into a form of yard art. Tires are a little bulky and awkward to work with, but they make very long-lasting planters. Paint the tire a light color. Dark colors, such as the tire's original black, tend to absorb heat from summer sun, which can harm the plants. If you want to skip the paint job, use trailing plants around the rim of the tire to cover most of its surface or use spreading or bushy plants in the ground around the perimeter.

unusual container

right and *below:* Tire planters make excellent focal points in herb gardens, cornerstones on patios, or simple circular beds in the middle of a small patch of lawn.

plants

1. verbena *bonariensis*
2. japanese blood grass
3. parrot's beak
4. 'aurea' moneywort
5. sweet alyssum
6. zinnia

1 **cut pattern** Use a standard automobile tire still attached to a rim for easiest handling. Truck and tractor tires, though spacious, prove harder to handle. Avoid radial tires, because they're too difficult to maneuver and to cut. Trace a scallop pattern with chalk around the sidewall of the tire before you begin cutting. Make the first and last scallops meet evenly at the beginning and the end. Using a strong, sharp knife with a serrated blade, carefully cut the pattern, as shown.

2 **turn inside out** Turn the tire over. With the cut side down, slide your gloved hands into the opening you cut in Step 1. Place a foot firmly on the rim of the tire and—with one hand pulling and the other pushing—start to turn the tire inside out. This takes some brute force and perhaps two people, depending on your strength. Continue pulling and pushing all around the tire until you have the inside facing out.

3 **trim and plant** Point the top edge up. Use tin snips or a pruner to trim the scalloped edge as you like.

Set the tire where you want it to be when planted. (You won't want to move it later.) Paint it any color you wish and let dry completely.

Fill with an enriched potting mix. Plant herbs, annuals, dwarf ornamental grasses, miniature roses, or a combination of any of these.

birdhouse planter

cost	make it	skill
$–$$	4–5 hours	moderate

you will need

birdhouse, as desired

15–20 cedar or asphalt shingles

3d finishing nails

2½-inch-long flathead nails

sheet moss

spanish moss

U–shape florist's picks

four 6-packs of plants

30 plants in 6-packs and 3–inch pots

for birds and you

Besides offering resting spots for feathered friends, birdhouses also make a delightful garden accent if you imagine their planting possibilities. With the addition of a custom roof and some moss, you'll create a place where small plants can spread their roots. Set the planted birdhouse in partial shade to protect it from the drying effects of direct sun. Remove spent flowers to keep plants producing new blooms. Replace plants every year; transplant hardy ivies and chrysanthemums to the garden.

flower sanctuary

right and *below:* An ordinary birdhouse becomes extraordinary when the roof overflows with flowers. A 2-inch-deep base provides just enough space to accommodate a few more plants.

plants

1 chrysanthemum

2 miniature rose

3 variegated ivy

4 impatiens

5 fern

1 roof Raise the birdhouse on the 2-inch tray by nailing it to a 2×4 support. Nail the 2×4 bottom to the tray. Cover the original roof with cedar or asphalt shingles by overlapping and attaching them using finishing nails. Allow an overhang on the sides. Overlap the shingles at the roof's apex. If you use cedar shingles, drill pilot holes before nailing, to prevent splitting the shingles. Hammer 2½-inch nails 2 inches apart in staggered rows, jutting up 1 inch, for attaching moss.

2 moss Soak sheet moss in water until it is thoroughly wet; wring out most of the water. Attach the moss to the roof by slipping it over and between the nails.

Immerse potted plants in a bucket of water mixed with a liquid fertilizer. A starter fertilizer that contains B vitamins helps plants resist transplant shock. Follow the package directions for the correct amount.

3 plant Remove plants from their pots and push the root ball of each onto one of the nails on the roof. Cover the bare soil with wet moss using florist picks. Fill the base of the birdhouse with potting mix and place plants along the edge. Tuck pieces of Spanish moss between the plantings for a decorative finish and to help keep the root balls from drying out.

Water plants gently every day or two—daily in hot, dry weather. Feed every other week with a liquid fertilizer.

yard & garden projects | **245**

classic–finish container

cost	make it	skill
$	weekend	moderate

you will need

- container, as desired
- flat latex paint: black and one contrasting color
- paintbrush
- latex liquid glaze
- rags
- clear sealant spray

faux verdigris

Using this simple technique of painting and dabbing, you'll give containers an aged, weathered look. All it takes is two coats of contrasting colors.

weathered look
right and *below:*
Simulate the real verdigris finish on metal pots that results from years of exposure to the elements.

plants

1 geranium
2 petunia
3 gerbera daisy
4 dusty miller

1 base coat Antique any surface, including terra-cotta, plastic, and metal. The technique looks best on pieces with cracks, crevices, and details. Do a trial run on the bottom of the pot so any mistakes you make won't show on the finished surface.

Begin by painting a base coat with one color of latex paint. Flat black latex paint, used here, gives a terra-cotta pot the look of a bronze urn with a verdigris finish. Allow the base coat to dry completely.

2 top coat Prepare the top coat by mixing a latex liquid glaze with a second color of latex paint. Use a ratio of about one part glaze to four parts paint. Apply the top coat (at left, a slightly gaudy aqua).

Latex paint dries fast, so paint only a small area at a time (about the size of a baseball card). Leave irregular edges, then blend them as you continue to paint, using the antiquing technique described below.

3 antiquing Immediately after you apply a section of top coat, wad up a rag and blot or dab the paint gently. Soften the edges first, then go over the middle. Move and remove the top coat until you achieve a look that you like.

When you have covered the entire surface, let the paint dry completely. Seal with three coats of clear sealant spray; allow the sealant to dry completely between the coats.

let there be light

Transforming your garden from a grow place into a showplace need not involve a bundle of money or a professional designer. Lighting demonstrates how easy and affordable garden decor can be.

lighten up Whether portable or more permanent, lighting enhances the garden's beauty and safety as well as extending its use after hours. Conjure enchanted evenings in your garden with lanterns, candleholders, and other night lighting. These inexpensive accents glow with personality, especially when placed at entryways, on tables, under eaves, in tree branches, and in other appropriate spots around the scene. Colorful and graceful, candlelight turns a garden into a party place. Twinkle lights add a bit of whimsy, especially when strung in unexpected ways around tabletops or along the rooftop of a garden shed.

time and place Low-voltage lighting offers an easy-to-install alternative when your goals include added security and safety. The placement of light fixtures and the direction of their beams help you achieve various artistic effects with your lighting design. These lighting techniques include uplighting to highlight surface details of trees, shrubs, and other objects; downlighting to mimic moonlight and cast ground shadows; and backlighting to accentuate the shapes of objects by highlighting them from behind.

lighting

night lights

Outdoor lighting woven through your garden adds warmth, magic, and glow. Use candles, string lights, torches, or lanterns. Amplify the brightening effect by siting reflective surfaces nearby, such as water or a gazing ball. White flowers and light-color surfaces also gleam with a subtle luminescence when accompanied by light.

Candles offer a simple but spellbinding touch. Before including candles in your garden, however, follow these basic safety tips:

- Keep a bucket of water, a garden hose, or a fire extinguisher nearby.
- Before handling metal or glass candle accessories, allow them to cool, or wear heat-resistant barbecue mitts.
- Trim candlewicks to ¼ inch before lighting.
- Place unenclosed candles away from leaves and flammable fabrics.
- Fit candles snugly in their holders.
- Store matches and lighters in a secure place away from open flames and children.
- When candles are not in use, store them indoors, or turn their containers over to prevent rain and dirt from accumulating.
- To remove melted wax from containers, store them in the freezer for two hours before gently prying off the wax. To remove soot, fill the container with hot, sudsy water; allow the container to soak for several hours before scrubbing it.
- Keep all lit candles out of the reach of children and pets.

floral flotilla

right: **Terra-cotta saucers filled with water, choice blooms, leaves, and floating candles make an attractive centerpiece. White candles work well with any color of flowers and foliage; keep plenty of candles on hand for the gardening season.**

dynamic duo
above left: Dragonfly string lights pair handsomely with tea lights.

buzz on
above: Linen bags, stamped with fabric ink and stuffed with plastic wrap, make white twinkle lights dazzle.

candles ahoy
left: Stand a twine-tied bouquet in a wide-mouth vase; add rocks, water, and floating candles for spectacular results.

lighting

lighten up

Set your garden aglow with innovative, inexpensive lighting. Candles, strings of lights, and lanterns add as much appeal as a skyful of twinkling stars. The soft illumination casts a hypnotic spell that's conducive to evening entertaining and late-night conversations.

If your night-lighting choices include candles, explore display options and use materials that you have on hand. Line the center of a table with glass-footed compotes or sherbet dishes filled with votives. Give new life to canning jars by covering the bottom with an inch or two of sand, small river rock, marbles, sea glass, or recycled glass; stand a small candle inside. Transform the jars into hanging lanterns by tightly wrapping wire around jar necks and twisting it to form a loop above the mouth of the jar. Burn citronella-scented candles for their reputed bug-repelling effects.

Shelter flames from wind by snuggling candles into deep containers or by slipping glass chimneys or patterned graters or colanders over lit candles.

Use oil lamps or lanterns whenever an evening calls for sustained lighting. Or rely on electric lights for hours-on-end illumination. String Chinese-style lanterns from gutters to light a walkway, taking care to purchase the right-size bulbs to fit inside the paper globes. Weave strings of twinkle lights around tree branches to add sparkle to the evening breeze. Outline a garden trellis, market umbrella, or fence with strings of lights to create a glimmering

fiery flowers

right: Fashion a tabletop water garden that glows after dark. Float water lettuce plants in a large enamel pan. Tuck 2-inch-round candles or tea lights into the center of each plant. Other potential candleholders include tulips, roses, or other large, floatable blooms. Snip off the stem (and inner petals of the roses) and nestle a tea light within the flower petals.

focal point. Stand lights among garden flowers and foliage for a magical glow.

Place lights to illuminate potentially treacherous footing, such as around a deck, along a path, or beside stairs. Place lights near seating and dining areas, either above head or below eye level to avoid bumps and glare.

For more decorating ideas with candles visit **www.bhg.com/ bkcandles**.

thrift-store glow

left: **Secondhand fixtures include tapers standing in a sand-filled watering can, bud-vase-shaded string lights, and wineglasses topped with shades from old gas lamps.**

twinkle lights

Low-cost strings of lights become rich with character when you dress bulbs in homemade lampshades. Slightly enlarge the drainage holes in 2-inch-wide terra-cotta pots by scraping them with a drill bit. One by one, remove bulbs, and slip each light fixture through the drainage hole. Replace the bulbs, and hang the lights. Vary the theme with shades made from aluminum foil cupcake holders, tiny baskets, or … be inventive!

yard & garden projects | **253**

low-voltage lights

luxurious lighting

Illumination enhances a garden room's usefulness after the sun sets. Electric outdoor lighting converts dark spaces and shadowy corners into inviting living areas. What's more, night lighting promotes sure footing as well as your home's security.

If you make safety and security your lighting goals, tuck various kinds of lights beside paths, into stair-step risers, and near outdoor seating. Select strong-beam bulbs to discourage intruders.

To cast a welcoming glow, choose low-voltage lights to bathe an entry area with gentle illumination. Look for easy-to-install low-voltage lighting kits at home centers or hardware stores or on the Internet. Install light-sensitive, photocell timers to switch lights on and off automatically at dusk and dawn. Instead of lighting all areas of your garden uniformly, use a variety of fixtures with different angles of light, such as dramatic uplighting and traditional downlighting. Arrange illumination to create patches of light and darkness. Plan your lighting for easy lightbulb changing. Install a switch in the house for convenient control of your landscape lights.

night lights

right and *far right:* **Choose functional and beautiful light fixtures, repeating the style throughout your landscape. For a dramatic effect, use strands of lights to outline a structure, such as a gazebo, a pergola, or an arbor. Ceiling lights brighten this gazebo's interior.**

installing low-voltage lights

1 lay the course Choose a low-voltage (typically 12-volt) lighting kit for economy, practicality, and ease of installation. Map the lighting route on paper; determine where you'll place the lamps. Following the manufacturer's directions, install the transformer (power) box on an outside wall near an outlet. Attach the low-voltage cable to the terminal screws on the transformer. Unwind the cable and lay it along the course for the lights.

2 complete the connections Position light fixtures along the length of cable. Snap the fixtures onto the cable. With most lighting kits, teeth in each fixture's connector pierce the cable to create the electrical connection. Attach anchoring stakes to fixtures. Plug the transformer into the outlet to survey light placement. Make any necessary adjustments, then spike fixtures into the ground. Vary lamp heights as desired. A higher position expands the cast of light; a lower position reduces it.

3 position the lights When you're satisfied with the height and position of your lights, bury the cable 2 to 4 inches deep (unless code requirements specify otherwise). To bury the cable, slit the turf with a spade, lift the sod, lay the cable underneath, and replace the sod. In planting beds or paths, cover the cable with mulch, bark, or gravel. For a hands-free switch that automatically turns lights on and off, choose a light-sensitive transformer or install an outdoor timer.

wooden lanterns

cost	make it	skill
$$–$$$	weekend	moderate

you will need

- low-voltage light set
- four cedar fence panels (see dimensions on plan, *opposite*)
- compass
- power drill
- jigsaw
- table saw
- exterior-grade wood glue
- 4d finishing nails
- no. 6 ¾-inch brass roundhead wood screws
- carpenter's square
- nail set
- sandpaper
- exterior varnish
- wood putty

night lights

Low-voltage outdoor lights are easy to install, and they add ambience, safety, and security to your landscape. But the garden-variety plastic fixtures could do with a makeover in wood.

Choose from four handsome wood-surround designs to dress up a light set (available from retail and mail-order sources) to suit your garden's style. Build the surrounds of weather-resistant wood such as cedar, redwood, or cypress. The plans (*opposite*) use standard cedar-fencing panels to construct surrounds that beautify the ordinary lights, transforming them into a decorative asset. If you don't feel up to the task of building the surrounds, hire a carpenter to make them for you. The low-voltage light set you purchase will determine the number of surrounds you'll need.

When installing the lanterns, bury the bottom 2 to 3 inches of the surrounds for stability, or secure them to a wooden stake hidden inside or on the back side of each surround.

lighting quartet

above: Choose from four lamp designs to make your softly glowing lanterns, featuring *(clockwise from left)* a plain pedestal style, a beveled cover, a chamfered surround, or a copper top.

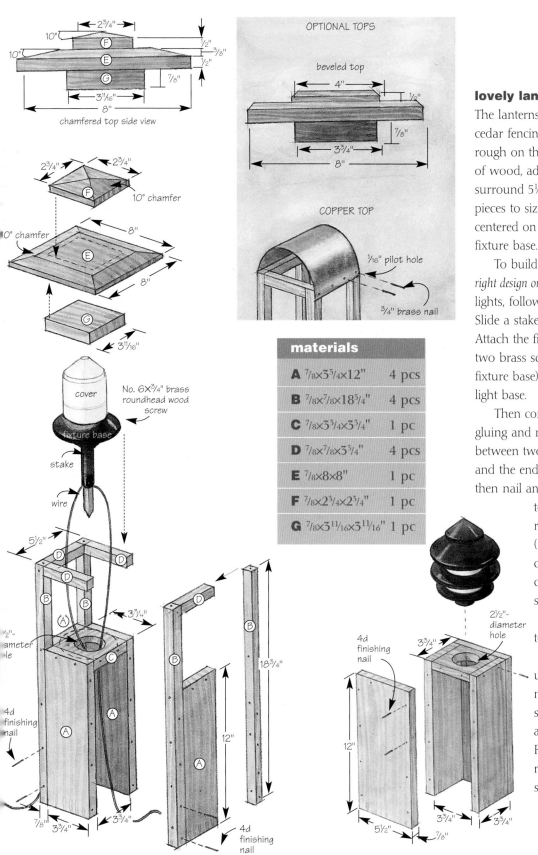

OPTIONAL TOPS

beveled top

4"

1/2"

3 3/4"

7/8"

8"

COPPER TOP

1/16" pilot hole

3/4" brass nail

2 3/4"

10°

10°

F

1/2"

3/8"

1/2"

E

G

7/8"

3 11/16"

8"

chamfered top side view

2 3/4"

2 3/4"

F

10° chamfer

10° chamfer

8"

E

8"

G

3 11/16"

cover

No. 6×3/4" brass roundhead wood screw

fixture base

stake

wire

5 1/2"

D

D

D

B

B

A

2"-diameter hole

C

3 3/4"

4d finishing nail

A

A

A

7/8"

3 3/4"

3 3/4"

D

B

B

A

18 3/4"

12"

4d finishing nail

4d finishing nail

2 1/2"-diameter hole

4d finishing nail

3 3/4"

12"

5 1/2"

7/8"

3 3/4"

3 3/4"

materials

A	7/8×3 3/4×12"	4 pcs
B	7/8×7/8×18 5/4"	4 pcs
C	7/8×3 3/4×3 3/4"	1 pc
D	7/8×7/8×3 3/4"	4 pcs
E	7/8×8×8"	1 pc
F	7/8×2 3/4×2 3/4"	1 pc
G	7/8×3 11/16×3 11/16"	1 pc

lovely lanterns

The lanterns (*opposite*) were built using 7/8-inch-thick cedar fencing, which is smooth on one side and rough on the other. If you use a different thickness of wood, adjust the dimensions to make each surround 5 1/2 inches square. Cut all the wood pieces to size. Mark a 2 1/2-inch-diameter hole centered on each lamp support (C) to fit the plastic fixture base. Cut the hole with a jigsaw.

To build the chamfer-style unit shown (*far right design on page 256*), first connect the wiring and lights, following the instructions in your light set. Slide a stake and fixture through the hole in part C. Attach the fixture base to the lamp support using two brass screws (predrill holes through each fixture base). Add the plastic cover to the light base.

Then construct the covered surrounds by gluing and nailing one side (A) and one rail (D) between two uprights (B), keeping the surfaces and the ends flush. Repeat to create a second panel, then nail and glue these two preassembled panels to the lamp support. Glue and nail the remaining two sides (A) and two rails (D) between the existing panels to complete the surround. Check the corners for a 90-degree angle. Use a nail set to countersink nails slightly

Build the tops last; cut chamfered tops using a table saw.

Sand the surrounds and their tops until smooth. Allow them to weather naturally, or apply an exterior finish such as spar varnish. If you use a finish, apply one coat and allow it to dry. Fill in the nail holes using wood putty matching the wood finish. Apply a second coat of finish.

blue glass votives

cost	make it	skill
$	2 hours	easy

sky blue

Pint-size canning jars, glazed with paint to match a garden's decorating scheme, provide pretty and low-cost candle lanterns. The blue-hue jars enhance the garden scene while protecting the candles from breezes.

A garden that gets the blues can be a pretty thing. Just coordinate all the accessories in your garden as shown with an easy-to-apply coat of paint, or match ready-made items. A single-color theme ties together incongruous pieces, from mismatched furniture to odd pots and other elements. Choose decorative fabrics and tableware featuring the same color.

Surround your color-drenched setting with flowers that bloom in complementary hues. In this case, yellow, orange, pink, and white make excellent plant companions for the blue scheme. If you're unsure what color to use, browse paint chips at your local home improvement or paint store.

hot stuff

right and *far right:* **Use long matches to light short candles tucked inside jars. Or use a handheld propane lighter with a long nozzle (often sold alongside grilling products).**

1 **gather jars** Select the containers you want as candleholders. Glass jars of any kind, vases, or deep bowls work well. Match candles to containers. Wide-mouth containers up to 6 inches tall can hold small pillar candles. Tea lights fit easily inside half-pint glass jars or shallow bowls. Use a wide, shallow disposable container, such as a plastic pot saucer, when glazing the glass containers.

2 **prepare the palette** Glaze your glassware with an acetone-base spray paint, because it will float on the water's surface. Fill the plastic saucer with water. Use a floral-type spray paint (Design Master No. 743, deep blue, *shown*), formulated for spraying color on fresh or dried flowers and available from a crafts store or floral supplier. Spray a light coat of paint on the water's surface.

3 **dip and swirl** Create the soft, mottled effect on the glass by dipping each container into the water and rotating it once to glaze it with paint. To avoid fingerprints, use tongs. Coating the glass with too much paint diminishes the glazed effect. This method is not suitable for tableware used for serving or eating; the paint won't hold up to repeated washings. To paint statuary with a similar effect, mist statues with water before spraying on paint.

yard & garden projects | **259**

paper lanterns

cost	make it	skill
$	3 hours	easy

you will need

- two lampshades with socket rings (per lantern)
- bolt cutter
- fabric seam binding
- corrugated paper
- scissors
- twine
- crafts glue
- metal clips
- twine
- colored paper
- votive candle holder
- votive candle

outdoor lighting

Decorate your garden with more than daytime enjoyment in mind. Handmade paper lanterns lit with votive candles cast a soft glow that's perfect for evenings among the flowers.

Gardeners rarely walk through their patches of tended earth during the day without stopping to pull a weed, straighten a stake, or snap off a dead bloom. It's not that the dirty-knees crowd is a compulsive bunch; it's that the garden is an ever-changing place, and the to-do list grows as quickly as the plants. It takes more than planting some cozy-cushioned seats in a strategic part of the garden to guarantee you'll stop to smell your roses. Night lighting offers an irresistible option. In the dim light, even the most obsessive gardener can't see any weeds to pull. Keep the lights low, and you'll discover the wonders of night in your garden. Allow yourself to sit back and savor the flowers' fragrance and the insects' evening songs.

candlelight and flowers

right: **Complement your glowing lanterns with a fragrant evening garden of moonflower, vining petunia, flowering tobacco, evening primrose, datura, and heliotrope.**

1 cut For each lantern, start with two lampshade frames (six-paneled or similar) equipped with socket rings. Remove the ring from one of the frames using bolt cutters. This frame forms the top of the lantern. Remove any material covering the shades, leaving bare frames. Place the frames' bottoms together and wrap with seam binding; secure the fabric by tying the ends. Make a lantern-panel template of cardboard and use it to cut medium-weight corrugated paper (from an art supply store).

2 glue Apply decoupage or pressed dried leaves and flowers to the insides of the panels. Before gluing, tie three lengths of twine to the top of the frame (where you removed the ring socket) spaced evenly apart. Tie the other three ends together in a knot. Use crafts glue to attach the paper panels to the top lampshade frame. Hold panels in place with metal clips until glue dries. Flip the lantern over and glue the panels in place on the second lampshade frame. Glue strips of colored paper in place to cover all the seams.

3 hang Set a votive candleholder in the socket ring; insert the candle. Hang lanterns from tree branches, a pergola, or an arbor using S-shape hooks. Trim excess twine to keep it safely away from candle flames. To reduce fire hazard, avoid using lanterns on windy evenings. Paper lanterns should not hang outdoors overnight. One night's dew can warp the paper.

sea-glass lantern

cost	make it	skill
$	½ hour	easy

you will need

- votive candle or tea light
- two clear glass cylindrical vases (one wider than the other)
- sea glass

just beachy

Add a little nightlife to your garden with an easy handcrafted candle that's elegant enough for the most formal indoor setting. The gentle light of a candle becomes a shimmering glow as it shines through a layer of frosty sea glass (pieces tossed, sculpted, and worn by waves).

For candles that won't go out as the evening breezes stir your garden, tuck them into deep containers that protect them from wind. Start with two cylindrical glass vases in graduated sizes, available from florist suppliers and crafts stores. Slip a votive candle inside the smaller cylinder, and place that inside the larger vase. Fill the spaces between the two cylinders with clear or colored sea glass, also available from crafts stores.

glassy glow

When the sun sets and the crickets begin to chirp, a handful of candles and a string of twinkle lights unlock the mystery of the evening garden. The real beauty of twilight garden illumination emerges as a small investment yields large results in light, charm, and unforgettable ambience.

carrying a torch

right and *opposite top:* The secret to keeping flames tamed to a gentle flicker in the garden is to protect them from the wind. Tuck candles into deep glass containers to shelter the flames.

more night lights

Float candles in a deep birdbath, or tuck votives or tea lights inside clear, colored, or frosted glass cups, lanterns, or lamps. Drape electric lights over shrubs, and wrap strings of lights around tree branches overhanging seating areas. Oil lamps burn the longest and strongest, providing a clear, steady flame for hours on end. Take care to wipe up any oil spills with a clean rag; carefully dispose of the rag to avoid a fire hazard.

chimney-cap lanterns

Turn inexpensive, galvanized chimney covers (available at hardware stores) into sleek, unusual lanterns. Spray-paint the chimney covers with exterior-grade enamel; let dry. Drill holes along the edge of the chimney cap from which to dangle stones. Wrap thin wire around smooth river stones and feed a wire through each hole; snip off any excess wire after you have wrapped and hung each stone. Center the chimney cap over a votive candle. The chimney cover will become extremely hot as the candle burns. Use heat-resistant mitts, or allow caps to cool completely before handling them. Avoid placing lanterns where children, guests, or pets might come in contact with them.

finishing touches

Personal touches transform a house into a home. In the garden, the same effect occurs when gardeners accessorize their outdoor spaces with decor that helps unwind the mind, soothe the soul, and delight the eye. Some of the most satisfying garden embellishments capitalize on natural resources—wind, water, and fire—or on found objects to enhance the beauty of life in the garden.

sincerely yours Embellish your garden with creative flourishes that make a personal statement. Express yourself with a collection of vintage artifacts or treasures from your travels. Whether you think of yourself as more of a gardener than a garden decorator, now's your chance to experiment with various touches.

Outdoor fabrics cater to comfort and maximize any style statement, whether vintage, Old World, or tropical. Choose from a wide selection of easy-to-sew fabrics that weather well as curtains, canopies, cushion covers, and more.

details, details Focus on sensory appeal, and you won't overlook any opportunity to apply details that help complete your garden settings. Choose artful elements that provide pleasure at a glance or a touch, or delight merely with their sound. Trickling water or tinkling wind chimes play melodies that will tickle your ears and mask neighborhood noise. Wind art that dances, spins, and bobs in a breeze proves pleasing; the more comical wind dancers may even incite a few giggles.

Splash a favorite color around your garden—on fences, cushions, and containers. Color ties together an eclectic setting, tastefully and artistically.

outdoor fabrics

1 **a stitch in time** Pamper yourself with creature comforts crafted from weather-worthy textiles. Choose fabrics according to projects, favoring blends made for outdoor use. For grill covers and table linens, choose soil- and stain-resistant materials for easy cleanup. Select lightweight fabrics for billowy curtains or graceful slipcovers. Choose heavier textiles that hang straight and tend not to blow for edging curtains, skirting a workbench, or covering furniture. Dark-color and patterned fabrics disguise dirt and stains easily. If you prefer solids, choose textured fabrics for pleasing results.

2 **pillow talk** Cover outdoor cushions in lively hue fabric that's made to resist moisture, stains, and mildew. Sew welt cord into the seams of pillows and cushions to improve their durability and give them a tailored look. Making cushion covers with zippers allows easy removal for washing. Select a nylon zipper over a metal one, which can corrode and stick. Or, for a nifty closure, install nickel-plated snaps. Stuff pillows with polyester fiberfill, which absorbs little moisture. Most cushions and pillows crafted with outdoor fabrics last for years. Extend that longevity by storing them under cover when not in use. If you want cushion ties to help keep them in place, sew two ties into the back corner seams of the cushion covers. Use either narrow strips of matching fabric or heavy ribbon to make the ties.

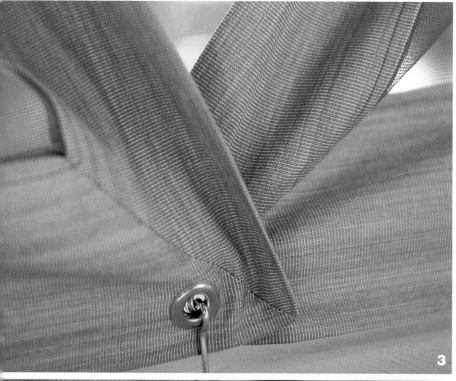

anchors away Invent your own
easy-to-install pulley system to hang cloth
draperies or screen and fabric panels (*left*)
on a porch, deck, or other outdoor structure.
First, make the panels by sewing a 4-inch-
wide fabric edging onto 60-inch-wide
fiberglass window screening (from a
hardware store or home center). Screw
hooks into a porch ceiling or overhead
beams to suspend individual panels. Slip
hooks through grommet holes you have
punched into the panel or curtain corners
with a grommet-making tool. Use nylon
laundry line and sailboat pulleys to raise,
lower, or draw back the drapes. To keep
a panel or drape raised or gathered to one
side, wrap the line around a cleat attached to
a railing or the floor. Peruse a marine supply
store for heavy-duty hardware such as
pulleys and cleats, which are made to
withstand the elements. Tuck weights into the
bottom edging or hem of drapes to minimize
their billowing when the wind blows.

on edge Experiment with different
edging treatments as you plan your fabric
accessories. A mitered corner, neatly sewn in
a contrasting fabric, adds a formal touch to
a tablecloth or floorcloth. Select oilcloth for
table toppers or floor coverings, and you
won't need to hem edges. Instead use pinking
shears to cut geometric edges, such as zigzags
or scallops. Stitch decorative trims to pillows
that suit your room's style: Use nylon fringe,
topstitching, rickrack, or leather seam binding.
Hire a professional to make your outdoor
fabric accessories if sewing isn't your forte.

outdoor fabrics: canopy

fresh-air fantasy

Modern outdoor fabrics withstand high humidity, drenching downpours, and glaring sun without fading or disintegrating. Swaths of fabric soften structures while adding a graceful curve, an alluring fold, or a cascade of touchable beauty.

Work textiles into your outdoor-room plans and reap the rewards of comfort and style. Fabric panels dangling like banners form billowing walls. Suspended in gravity-defying trapeze-artistry fashion, a fabric ceiling provides a canopy perfect for shielding guests from bright sun or light rain. In a romantic hideaway (*right*), an easy-to-stitch hanging canopy provides privacy and shelter under branches and leaves. Opulent prints dress up a mundane outdoor table and cover cushions with verve. Slipcovers give everyday chairs an exotic look.

Find awning materials at fabric shops and outdoor furniture stores. Look for polyester, acrylic, or nylon fabrics that promise protection against ultraviolet light. Stitch your creations together with polyester or nylon thread, which is designed to withstand the elements.

table for two

right: **Coordinated fabrics set the tone for a cozy getaway area. A wrought-iron candle chandelier and matching candlestands heighten the romantic mood. Open-air walls let the serenades of birds, bugs, and breezes flow through.**

overhead hangups

Casting shade or catching raindrops, the fabric ceiling unfurls among the trees. Determine your canopy dimensions based on the size of your seating ensemble. Sew a decorative edge of a contrasting, heavy-duty fabric, which will help the canopy weather wind. Place nickel-plated grommets into each corner, and hang the fabric from nylon rope attached to trees or tent stakes. Remove any leaf litter or twigs that fall onto the fabric from trees overhead.

sheer slipcover

Sheer netting slipcovers drape ordinary metal-frame garden chairs with formal fancy. Find mosquito netting (made for outdoor use) at fabric and bedding stores. Place 2 to 3 yards of fabric over each chair. Cut tiny slits in the netting and thread the seat cushion ties through the cuts; tie cushions to chair frames with snug bows.

a fetching sketch

Plan your outdoor retreat with a site in mind. Inventory the location, taking note of branches that might serve as supports for the canopy and overhead lighting. Employ tent poles or sturdy stakes to uphold ends of the canopy that lack limb braces. Change the atmosphere altogether by switching fabrics. Trade the tailored look for bold tropical prints or bright, angular south-of-the-border designs.

art:collections

garden gatherings

Collections turn passion into personal style. Hand tools or painted pots become a handsome garden display when artfully arranged en masse. Added to the garden as a group, small items have a big impact that reflects your personality.

To curate a collection, track down garden treasures at estate or house sales or at garden shops. Once you've chosen the object of your desire (such as folk art, star-shape items, or bunnies of any sort), keep an eye out when you travel and tell your friends what you're collecting.

Hunting for collectibles should be part of the fun, so think twice before setting your sights on obscure or pricey antique pieces, such as green-handle tools or handwoven wattle fences, which may be frustratingly hard to find.

inside out

above: Architectural features, such as finials, are fun to collect. Part of the beauty of a painted wood piece is the way it cracks and peels with time. Protect wooden treasures by displaying them beneath an eave or on a porch.

roosting wall

right: A wall that beckons like a blank canvas is dressed up with a flock of vintage birdcages and birdhouses.

clay on display
left: Terra-cotta plaques, pots, and sculptures emanate desert style with their earthen tones. Display Mexican terra-cotta away from the elements; it deteriorates when exposed to weather.

used but useful
below: Start a collection with a gathering of functional items, such as galvanized watering cans and vintage pots. Display them on an accessible-but-artful fence shelf.

collective effort
Decorative items with collectible potential abound, depending on what strikes your fancy. Select objects that can withstand weather. Consider these possibilities:

- architectural salvage
- metal garden furniture
- old signs
- pickets
- vintage metal riding toys
- weather vanes

art: garden characters

a motley crew

Populate your garden with a crew of folk-art creatures, from scarecrows and mannequins to wildlife replicas. Although fanciful topiaries or cleverly outfitted statues won't guard your crops from pillaging birds, they will inject a little humor into the growing scene. Replicas of people can keep wildlife on the wary side, but eventually animals figure out that the lady standing by the garden gate never moves. To shoo pesky critters that feast on the fruits of your labor, try this trio of scarecrow-building tricks:

movement Give your scarecrow moving elements. Cloth streamers or mylar ties flutter in the wind and startle animals that wander near your garden patch or scratch within the plantings.

light Flickering light agitates birds and discourages them from landing among your plantings. Give scarecrows hair made from reflective mylar tape; string aluminum pie tins or pocket mirrors from their hands to keep animals on the move.

sound Animals are scared by anything that rattles with the wind, such as aluminum pie tins full of dry beans, cast-off maracas, a string of hard plastic objects, or a fluttering pinwheel.

scared silly
right: **A fence post becomes a folksy scarecrow with the addition of wooden-pole arms and an inverted sap-bucket head. Black fabric streamers keep birds wary. An Indian-corn necklace adds a natural touch.**

potshard princess

left: Folk-art people with larger-than-life dimensions score big as garden focal points. This beauty, bedecked in white lights and clothed in potshards, braces her arms into a tray that can hold either plants or birdseed.

pretend pond

below: Topiary herons, turtle, and frog guard a make-believe water garden. Blue stones substitute for water in this whimsical pond.

art: papier-mâché sculpture

cost	make it	skill
$	weekend	easy

you will need

- balloon or chicken wire
- masking tape
- shredded newspaper, junk mail
- powdered cellulose or papier-mâché paste
- blender or food processor
- linseed oil

paper art

Elevate recycling to an art form by turning your piles of junk mail and old newspapers into garden sculpture with a stone look. Papier-mâché provides an easy, inexpensive way to add your handiwork to the garden.

Start by choosing a design and building an armature, or a framework, for your sculpture. Use a balloon as the armature for a head, a sun, or any spherical shape. For other shapes, such as angels, animals, or obelisks, mold chicken wire into a representative shape. Tape sheets of paper over the framework to form a smooth surface.

Shred junk mail and newspaper; place the paper in a tub of water (an old plastic dishpan works well). Soak the paper until it is saturated; then pour off the water. Mix approximately 1 quart of moist paper and 1 ounce of powdered cellulose, or papier-mâché paste (from an art supply store), in a blender or food processor. Adjust the proportions of cellulose and moist paper until you have a thick paste resembling the consistency of oatmeal; a bit more water may be needed to achieve a workable consistency.

Mold the mixture onto your armature. Sculpt contours on the piece and allow the papier-mâché to dry; then add layers to build dimension. Once the sculpture is complete and dry, waterproof it by brushing on linseed oil. Reapply linseed oil annually to extend the life of your art.

guardian angels
left: Angelic creations, made from junk mail and flour paste, keep watch over the garden. Balanced on cocktail stirrers, wire, and other found objects, these winged wonders are painted with plastic paint commonly used by electricians, which makes them waterproof.

unforgettable face
left: This life-size sculptural beauty—constructed from recycled paper and cellulose paste—withstands weather with a waterproof seal. Inspiration for three-dimensional designs abounds in books about classical architecture, cultural art forms, and ancient civilizations.

plant markers

cost	make it	skill
$	weekend	moderate

you will need

⅝-inch–diameter willow or other twigs

piece of birch bark, a cedar shake, a thin board, or metal flashing

½-inch copper nails

hammer

acrylic paint

fine artist's brush

1-inch paintbrush

polyurethane sealant

rustic settings

Natural materials belong in a garden. Whether you eventually plan to build an arbor, a fence, a rustic table, or a bench from twigs and fallen trees, start with something simple, such as these garden signs. Artistic ability is not required: A few imperfections go hand in hand with the sign's rough-hewn look.

finishing touch

right: **A charming plant marker is fun and easy to make.**

1

frame Gather willow or other twigs or round up prunings from your yard or a neighbor's. For best results, use straight twigs about ⅝ inch in diameter. Cut four pieces to make the frame: for example, two 3-inch-long pieces for the ends and two 6-inch-long pieces for the top and bottom of the frame. Cut a 12-inch-long piece for a stake. Using ½-inch copper nails, fasten the twigs together by driving a nail through a long piece and into the end of a short piece.

2

canvas Cut the piece on which you will paint from birch bark (from a fallen tree only), a cedar shake, a thin board, or metal flashing. Cut it to fit the outer dimensions of the frame. Nail the piece to the back of the frame using copper nails.

3

stake Nail a 12-inch-long twig to the back of the frame to make a stake, allowing the top of the stake to extend an inch or two above the sign.

4

paint Using acrylic paint and a fine artist's brush, paint the name of a plant or a general term, such as "Herbs," on the sign. If you're uncomfortable painting freehand, lightly pencil in the word or words before applying the paint. Let the paint dry completely (at least 1 hour).

With a 1-inch paintbrush, coat the sign, including the ends of the stake, with polyurethane sealant. Let the sealant dry for at least 24 hours, then apply a second coat.

wind

art in motion

Harness the breeze to decorate your garden with delightful motion and sound. The parts and pieces of three-dimensional wind art come to life, singing and dancing in the garden. Puffs of wind transform sometimes-still sculptures into dynamic mobiles.

Part of the fun of adding wind-propelled embellishments to the garden is choosing among a whirligig, wind sock, wind chime, or other feature. Choose sculptures to suit your garden's style and size, as well as your budget. Look for solidly constructed features. Copper, glass, brass, acrylic, mylar laminate, and wooden pieces are usually durable. A weatherproofed piece is best. Select a

on the wing

right: **As a counterweighted sculpture, this hummingbird balances atop a sturdy metal pole, bobbing, swiveling, and adding playful motion to the garden.**

spin art

below: **Brass and copper marry in a metal sculpture that swings with a puff of wind. The most dynamic wind-driven rigs feature many movable parts, such as this coiled-and-cupped wind catcher.**

volcanic music

left: **Obsidian, a dark glass formed from molten lava, plays a tinkling tune when strummed by a breeze. To prevent damage, hang glass chimes in a protected location.**

wind propellers

below: **Turn your woodworking talents loose to create a whirligig that's intriguing and colorful. Paint wind-driven items in hues to match your garden's palette.**

sculpture that offers a distinct movement, such as whirling, spinning, swiveling, or rocking. Secure your wind art with mounting hardware (if provided with the piece), a metal stake, or nylon string.

music in the air

Wind chimes take a garden into another dimension. When choosing chimes, consider their sound and appearance. Select traditional metal tube chimes to play exquisitely harmonized chords. For a more exotic look and sound, hang bamboo pipes that resonate with mellow notes or seashells that chatter in the breeze. Glass sings a melodic song; ceramic and polished stones resound with pleasant pitches.

Hang wind chimes in a high, exposed spot, such as under house eaves, for the most constant music. Locate chimes in a somewhat protected spot and shorten the hanger to diminish their sound, or place them strategically in your garden to keep you alerted to the weather. Hang wind chimes outdoors year-round, but be considerate of your neighbors' hearing when you place the chimes.

On the softer side, consider a flag, wind sock, or wind spinner. Typically made from plastic or cloth, they flutter or whirl in rippling color. Those with permanently dyed, military-grade polyester or nylon threads resist heat and light for the longest wear and least tear. Dangle banners and flags from a pole that includes an antitangling wrap; or hang them from the eave of an outbuilding. Preserve your fabric art by storing it indoors over winter if you live in a region with a harsh climate.

wind: chimes & weather vanes

cost	make it	skill
$	2 hours	easy

you will need

- discarded silver cutlery, including one fork
- small sledgehammer
- anvil, wooden block, or similar surface
- vise–grip pliers
- needle–nose pliers
- drill
- heavy fishing line

a true tuning fork

Take cutlery to the trees by making a wind chime. Pure silver plays the prettiest tune; gather it at thrift stores and secondhand shops. Collect spoons, knives, or forks; each piece plays a different tone. For instance, soup spoons sound baritone; forks trill lighter notes.

Flattened pieces play the loveliest melodies. Pound each piece with a small sledgehammer on a hard surface such as a solid wooden block or an anvil to flatten it. Drill a hole in the top end of each piece of silverware. For the chime support, bend the outer tines of a fork, as shown (*right*), curling each end into a tiny loop. Use fishing line to attach each of the dangling pieces to the fork loops.

silverware songs
right: Let the wind play chimes with cast-off cutlery. Mix silverware for a merry melody. Hang the creation where it will be enjoyed most.

ride the wind

Before high-tech radar and 24-hour weather channels, people kept track of weather with clues from nature. Today, meteorologists track the weather for most folks, using sophisticated equipment, giving their best predictions about what nature has in store.

Glean your own weather wisdom from something as simple as the wind. Install a few wind-driven devices, and begin your own prognostications. Or watch for more subtle clues. For instance, according to weather lore and science, when the wind incites leaves to turn and show their backs, rain is on the way. If rain comes first and wind second, it will be a severe storm, so pack up your gear and head inside. If you spot yellow skies at sunset, a still day will follow. If you see halos around the sun or moon, it means rain or snow will come soon (the halo is formed by ice crystals in the air).

weather art
above left: **A windmill adds motion to the garden and informs of weather changes. Traditional farm elements, such as towering windmills and weather vanes, bring vintage character to gardens.**

gusty clues
left: **Add a weather vane to your garden and watch what the wind direction reveals about incoming weather (see if your weather predictions improve).**

water

wet and wonderful

Water represents such an integral part of gardening that its possibilities might be overlooked. Water enhances garden decor with pleasing attributes, including sound, light reflection, and motion.

Still water in a reflective pool adds allure to any garden setting. Its depth mirrors the sky and provides mysterious appeal. With plants or not, a quiet pool creates a cool, soothing atmosphere. Make the most of the water's calming effect by placing seating nearby. Poke garden torches in nearby soil or float candles on the water's surface to multiply the flames' reflective dance.

Work water into your garden's decorating scheme by adding a containerized feature or a pond, a stream, or a waterfall. The sound of moving water, whether it splashes, trickles, or bubbles, promotes a sense of tranquillity.

Create a simple recirculating fountain in a watertight container. In a small garden, use a jar or bowl fountain that overflows into a belowground basin, or an elegant wall fountain that spouts into a container below it. A traditional tiered fountain or spouting statuary suits a large or formal garden.

A low, jet-type fountain splashing over pebbles and into an underground reservoir suits almost any garden and attracts wildlife, such as birds and dragonflies. It provides a safe water feature for a garden where children play. An added bonus is the rainbows that form when sunlight strikes the airborne water droplets. Ordinarily, however, you'll

wacky water

right: **Here's a leaky faucet you won't want repaired. The secret of this recirculating fountain is a small submersible pump inside the watering can that pumps water to a pipe running through a hole drilled near the base of the can and attaches to a spigot. A screen placed over the hole inside the can catches debris.**

want to locate your water feature in a partly shady place to prevent evaporation and slow the breeding of bacteria.

The sound of a fountain can drown out traffic noise. However, strive for balance. Avoid creating a water feature that sounds like Niagara Falls.

If you're concerned that a constant water supply will attract proliferating mosquitoes, take a preventive tack. Add a couple of goldfish to a pond, pool, or containerized feature; they eat mosquito larvae. Or float a mosquito control ring (available commercially) on the water. It kills mosquito larvae as it dissolves over the weeks but won't harm fish, plants, or people.

garden reflections
above left: A water mirror reflects plants and sky. Choose an elegant container, paint the interior midnight blue, and fill it to the brim.

rain-chain tunes
left: A resin-sealed bamboo gutter catches rain that strums the chain in watery tones.

water

water pots

Water decor becomes more affordable and meaningful when you design a dripping, gushing, or splashing fountain for your garden. Select a large container and design a fountain to fit your garden style. If you want to install it yourself and have not dealt with plumbing or electrical projects before, try making a simple trickling fountain to boost your confidence before you tackle larger-scale water features.

terra-cotta trickle

right: **This streaming fountain celebrates the beauty of classic water jars. Because this fountain cannot sustain freezing temperatures, the water must be drained and the jars stored indoors before cold weather arrives.**

artfully colored
left: A small, contained fountain nestles into a corner of the patio and splashes throughout the summer. Silvery lamb's-ears contrasts with the blue tones of the Japanese pot and flat-bottom bowl.

water on the move
below left: A copper sculpture comes to life, swirling, spraying, and creating kinetic water art when attached to a garden hose. Look for sprinkler designs that feature copper fixtures, several spinning parts, and even reflective glass baubles.

asian touch
below: Pair a bamboo pipe with a stone bowl to make water music in your garden. Adjust the trickling water to a pace that's pleasing; fill the basin with pebbles to modify the sound.

yard & garden projects | **285**

water: fountains

water wizardry

The sight and sound of a gurgling fountain affect the human psyche. Muscles relax, breathing deepens, and thoughts wander. Fountains foster a sense of well-being and tranquillity.

Soothe yourself with the magic of splashing water by starting small. Try a prefabricated tabletop fountain that nestles neatly into a corner of your deck or patio. If you're handy and adventurous, tackle building your own bubbling fountain. Easily adapt the project on pages 288 and 289 to construct a fountain in a container without a reservoir. Alternatively, search locally for artists who craft fountains from hand-cast concrete poured on wire forms, such as the columns shown *opposite.*

A fountain acts as a focal point and enhances a setting. Make fountains part of existing or planned seating areas. Use them as the anchor for a new garden area. Or place them near bedroom windows, where the trickling water plays a nightly lullaby.

While laying electrical lines for your fountain, wire the area for night lighting too. Fountains become almost mystical when lit from underwater at night using submersible halogen light fixtures. If working with electricity makes you nervous, hire an electrician. Keep costs down by digging the trenching and purchasing the project supplies.

pond trios

right: **This small but alluring pond combines a fountain and a stone bridge with a nearby tub full of water lilies to create a sublime aquatic scene.**

bold boulder
above left: Plumb
a granite rock for
a watery show. Find a
choice specimen at a
quarry. Hire a water-
garden specialist to
do the rest.

gentle shower
above: Recycle
a bathtub into a
fountain—complete
with a mossy duck!

trickling columns
left: A group of piped
concrete pedestal
fountains, topped
with urns of moisture-
loving plants,
makes an unusual
vertical feature.

water: urn fountain

cost	make it	skill
$$$	weekend	moderate

you will need

- container (concrete pot, urn, etc.)
- small submersible pump
- PVC pipe
- marine silicone sealant
- metal grate or mesh
- reservoir
- flexible two-layer PVC pond liner
- bricks or flat stones
- plastic electrical conduit
- ground fault circuit interrupter (GFCI) outlet
- assorted river rocks or cobblestones

backyard bubbler

A fountain brings multiple rewards to any garden. It requires minimal space and adds sound and movement. Trickling water helps mask nearby traffic noise and attracts birds, which bring color and ear-pleasing birdsong to the scene. Involve the whole family in the project and you will create a beautiful water feature for all to enjoy.

where to begin

First, select a vessel for your fountain. Find a one-of-a-kind container at an estate sale or a country auction or in your own garage. Consider concrete, ceramic, fiberglass, or plastic pots from a local garden center. You'll need to apply concrete sealer to a concrete pot. When purchasing the container, ask if it is watertight.

think bigger

right: Instead of settling for a basic fountain spray head, add a stately urn to your pond's aeration plan.

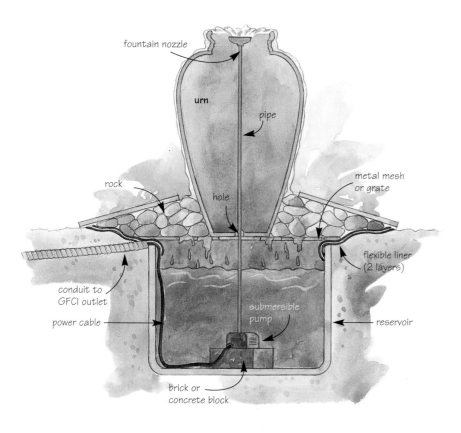

fountain nozzle

urn

pipe

rock

hole

metal mesh
or grate

flexible liner
(2 layers)

conduit to
GFCI outlet

power cable

submersible
pump

reservoir

brick or
concrete block

simple setup

The fountain sits above a reservoir of water. This water can be a pond (*opposite*) or an underground, rock-covered pool (*below left* and in the drawing, *left*). Build a reservoir large enough to capture all the water held in your urn (or similar container) and then some, because it bubbles over into the reservoir. Make the reservoir wider than the urn. A plastic tub works well. Spread two layers of flexible pond liner beneath the surrounding rocks and into the basin to help contain splashing water. Set the submersible pump on a brick or concrete block in the reservoir. Place the metal grate over the reservoir, making sure it's level.

power and water

Ensure that the hole in the bottom of your container accommodates the pipe from the pump. Use a masonry bit on a power drill to enlarge the hole if necessary. Run the pipe through the hole; seal around the pipe with marine silicone.

Install a weatherproof power outlet at least 4 feet away from the fountain. Install a ground fault circuit interrupter (GFCI) outlet in an existing outdoor outlet; or have a GFCI outlet installed by an electrician to prevent shorts and outages in your household circuitry. Run electrical wiring from the GFCI outlet through a conduit and a trench excavated beneath the flexible liner. Connect the power cord from the submersible pump to the wiring or to the outlet.

Set the container in place with the water delivery pipe attached to the pump. Test the pump before proceeding. Make adjustments in the spout height to control the fountain's water jet. When the fountain is running, the top of the pipe should be just below water level. Add stones to cover the metal grate. Run the fountain continually or whenever you desire. Check the water level frequently, adding water as needed.

bargain fountain

left: This ugly-duckling garage-sale find becomes a swan of a fountain and provides instant atmosphere with the sound of sheeting water.

cost	make it	skill
$$–$$$	weekend	moderate

you will need

- 22×32-inch ceramic pot
- 23-inch metal manger basket
- sheet plastic
- 23-inch coconut-husk basket liner
- 50-quart bag of potting mix
- potted plants, as desired
- three 48-inch bamboo stakes
- small water pump
- 24-inch bamboo water spout

making music

The sound of water trickling or pouring from a fountain or a spout masks obtrusive noises and creates natural, soothing music. Place a simple, Asian-style bamboo spout in a pot to bring that melody up close in your garden. Set tropical or subtropical plants in a container at the edge of the water garden. Or use dwarf and floating pond plants, which sit in the water. Bring tropical and subtropical plants indoors for the winter. The pot should be protected from freezing as well. Floating pond plants survive cold weather in more temperate climates if the water garden is deep enough, but to be safe, overwinter them indoors. Alternatively, set up the potted water garden indoors and enjoy it year-round.

plants

1 plectranthus

2 jasmine

3 ornamental sweet potato vine

4 helichrysum 'lemon licorice'

5 lemongrass

6 fern

Though the sound of gently splashing water provides a source of contentment for many, the fountain and pump are optional features for a potted water garden. Plants are optional, too, for that matter. You may prefer to start with a large container of water that's quietly reflective. If so, keep algae under control by cleaning the container and replacing the water in it every couple of weeks. If you decide that you'd enjoy the entertainment, add a pump and fountain to your water garden. If you wish, add plants later

plants and water

left and *opposite:* Water pouring from the bamboo spout doesn't disturb the plants here because they grow in a container (a manger basket) set securely on the rim of the ceramic pot. Colorful lilies float at the edge of the pond as a decorative touch.

water: potted water garden

1 **container and plants** Select a large container that holds about 35 gallons of water. A glazed ceramic pot works beautifully, but resin or fiberglass containers hold water too. The subtropical plants shown here are meant to sit in a container at the water's edge; they must be wintered indoors. If you prefer pond plants that dwell in the water, choose from those listed at *right*. Their containers are set directly in the water on bricks to achieve the appropriate depth.

2 **basket** Line the manger basket with a sheet of plastic, such as a lawn bag, and line that with the coconut-husk liner made to fit the frame. Add 3 inches of potting mix.

3 **plant** Remove plants from their nursery pots and arrange them in the planter. Place the largest plants in the center. Arrange the remaining plants evenly in the container, situating low-growing plants at the manger's edge. Sprinkle potting mix between the plants and to cover the root balls. Top off the plantings with 2 inches of mix.

Make a tepee to support the climbing plants, starting with two of the bamboo stakes. Push a stake into the soil at each end of the basket, then wire together the top ends of the stakes.

Cut the third bamboo stake in half and wire the half-length to the straight side of the basket and the tops of the other stakes, to add stability and to complete the tepee.

1

2

3

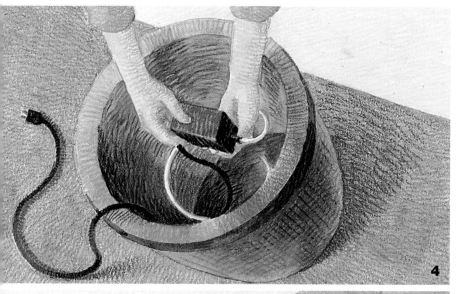

pump Before filling the pot with water, move it to the desired location; you won't be able to move the pot when it's full of water. Choose a spot that receives morning sun.

> Set a small water pump to the desired rate of flow. Place it in the bottom of the ceramic pot and drape the electrical cord over the side of the pot. The plants will conceal the cord. Connect the vinyl tubing at the base of the bamboo spout to the pump. Place the bamboo spout across the middle of the pot, with its ends resting on the rim.

4

finish Set the planter at one side of the pot, behind the bamboo spout. Fill the pot with water to just past the bottom of the planter. Slide the bamboo spout next to the front of the planter. Plug the pump into a three-prong grounded (GFCI) outlet. If the water flows too swiftly or too gently from the spout, experiment with the rate of flow on the pump to arrive at a desired level.

5

> Water plants when the soil feels dry, and fertilize once a month. In hot weather, top off the water in the pot as needed. In cold climates, dismantle the water garden in late fall, or bring the garden indoors for winter.

4

5

great plants for potted water gardens

■ arrowhead	■ parrot's feather
■ caladium	■ siberian iris
■ canna	■ sweet flag
■ duckweed	■ water clover
■ dwarf cattail	■ water fern
■ dwarf papyrus	■ water hyacinth
■ harlequin flower	■ water lettuce
■ miniature water lily	■ water snowflake

fire

fired up

Crackling flames, twinkling stars, and the
wonderfully soothing scent of wood smoke
provide the threads that weave unforgettable
memories. Make your home the destination of
choice for family and friends with a fire pit or an
outdoor fireplace.

Situate any fireplace well away from structures,
tree canopies, and neighbors who might be
troubled by smoke. Surround it with smooth
fireproof surfaces to eliminate tripping hazards.
Line a fire pit with firebrick, which withstands high
heat. Include a drain so water doesn't accumulate
and a lid that's flush with the ground to cover the
pit when not in use. Before you break ground,
check local building ordinances. If you can't burn
leaves in your area, you can't build a backyard fire
legally, no matter how well-contained it is.

freestanding fireplace

below: **A common sight in desert gardens,
the terra-cotta chiminea has roots in Mexico
as a compact, patio-warming fireplace ideal for
limited spaces.**

entertainment center

above: A fire pit in the backyard can make stargazing and storytelling favored family activities.

focus on comfort

left: A traditional fire pit goes upscale when surrounded with comfortable chairs. Extend the cushions' lives by storing them indoors when not in use.

Once you've cooked over open flames, you'll never want to go back to traditional grilling. Plan your fire pit with cooking in mind. Find commercially available barbecue hardware that fits the fire pit. Consider adding a grill rack, stainless-steel rotisserie, or whatever gadgets your grilling gourmet likes to use. Custom-built equipment is available, but pricey, through local machinists.

A raised stone wall offers simple but effective seating around a fire pit. If you prefer to use more comfortable seating, such as chairs with backs and cushions, set them far enough from the fire to minimize dangers from heat or sparks.

Find more decorating ideas for your garden at **www.bhg.com/bkgardenprojects**.

resources

art for the garden

Ancient Graffiti
52 Seymour St.
Middlebury, VT 05753
888/725-6632
www.ancientgraffiti.com

Garden Artisans
Rt. 1, Box 1079-Q5,
Townsend, GA 31331
912/437-2270
www.gardenartisans.com

Garden Smiles; George Carruth
211 Mechanic St.
Waterville, OH 43566
419/878-5412
www.carruthstudio.com

Sunspots Studio
202 S. Lewis St.
Staunton, VA 24401
540/885-8557
www.sunspots.com

bird supplies

Audubon Workshop
5200 Schenley Pl.
Lawrenceburg, IN 47025
812/537-3583
www.audubonworkshop.com

Duncraft
102 Fisherville Rd.
Concord, NH 03303
800/593-5656
www.duncraft.com

Heartwood, Architecture for the Birds
P.O. Box 298
Star, MS 39167
601/845-6530
www.heartwood-online.com

book

Making Bentwood Trellises, Arbors, Gates & Fences
Long Creek Herb Farm
P.O. Box 127
Blue Eye, MO 65611
417/779-5450
www.longcreekherbs.com

concrete stain

H & C Concrete Products
The Sherwin-Williams Co.
101 Prospect Ave. NW
Cleveland, OH 44115
800/474-3794
www.sherwin-williams.com

containers

Classic Garden Ornaments, Ltd.
Longshadow Gardens
83 Longshadow Ln.
Pomona, IL 62975
618/893-4831
www.longshadow.com

Frontgate
5566 West Chester Rd.
West Chester, OH 45069
800/626-6488
www.frontgate.com

A Garden of Distinction
5819 Sixth Ave. S.
Seattle, WA 98108
206/763-0517
www.agardenofdistinction.com

Stonesmith Garden Vessels
P.O. Box 713
Cambria, CA 93428
805/927-3707
www.stonesmith.com

Tierra International
P.O. Box 710
Jasper, IN 47547-0710
888/812-3384
www.tierraint.com

copper sprinklers

BirdBrain, Inc.
P.O. Box 130265
Ann Arbor, MI 48113
734/483.4536
www.birdbrain.com

everything gardening (furniture, ornaments, structures, containers, hardgoods, tools)

Charleston Gardens
61 Queen St.
Charleston, SC 29401
800/469-0118
www.charlestongardens.com

Frontgate
5566 West Chester Rd.
West Chester, OH 45069
800/626-6488
www.frontgate.com

Gardeners Eden
17 Riverside St.
Nashua, NH 03062
800/822-9600
www.gardenerseden.com

Garden Pals
3825 Manitou Ct.
Mira Loma, CA 91752
800/666-4044
www.gardenpals.com

Gardener's Supply Co.
128 Intervale Rd.
Burlington, VT 05401
888/833-1412
www.gardeners.com

Kinsman Co. Inc.
P.O. Box 428
Pipersville, PA 18947
800/733-4146
www.kinsmangarden.com

Peaceful Valley Farm Supply
P.O. Box 2209
Grass Valley, CA 95945
888/784-1722
www.groworganic.com

Smith & Hawken
P.O. Box 431
Milwaukee, WI 53201-0431
800/940-1170
www.smithandhawken.com

Worm's Way
7850 N. Highway 57
Bloomington, IN 47404
800/274-9676
www.wormsway.com

fabrics & cushions (for outdoor use)
Outdoor Fabrics
P.O. Box 160466
Miami, FL 33116
800/640-3539
www.outdoorfabrics.com

Plow & Hearth
P.O. Box 6000
Madison, VA 22727-1600
800/627-1712
www.plowhearth.com

Sunbrella
Glen Raven Custom Fabrics
1831 N. Park Ave.
Glen Raven, NC 27217-1100
336/221-2211
www.sunbrella.com

fencing
Hoover Fence Co.
P.O. Box 563
Newton Falls, OH 44444
330/358-2335
www.hooverfence.net

Lyric Japanese Antiques
8705 15th Ave N.W.
Seattle, WA 98117
206/782-4062
www.lyricjapanese.com

Mid Atlantic Vinyl Products
P.O. Box 41985
Fredericksburg, VA 22404
800/978-4695
www.mvp97.com

fire pits & patio fireplaces
Exterior Accents
9931-B Rose Commons Dr.
Huntersville, NC 28078
888/551-5211
www.exterior-accents.com

Final Touches
115 Morris St., P.O. Box 2557
Blowing Rock, NC 28605
877/506-2741
www.finaltouches.com

Fire Science, Inc.
8350 Main St.
Williamsville, NY 14221
716/633-1130
www.fire-science.com

fountains & supplies
Beckett Corp.
5931 Campus Circle Dr.
Irving, TX 75063
888/232-5388
www.888beckett.com

Stone Forest
P.O. Box 2840
Santa Fe, NM 87504
888/682-2987
www.stoneforest.com

Hughes Water Gardens
25289 S.W. Stafford Rd.
Tualatin, OR 97062
503/638-1709; 800/858-1709
www.watergardens.com

Springdale Water Gardens
340 Old Quarry Lane
P.O. Box 546
Greenville, VA 24440-0546
800/420-5459
www.springdalewatergardens.com

Stone Forest
P.O. Box 2840
Santa Fe NM, 87504
888/682-2987
www.stoneforest.com

fruit trees for espalier
Miller Nurseries
5060 West Lake Rd.
Canandaigua, NY 14424-8904
800/836-9630
www.millernurseries.com

Stark Bros.
P.O. Box 10
Louisiana, MO 63353
800/325-4180
www.starkbros.com

resources

furniture

Gloster Furniture, Inc.
606 Broad St. P.O. Box 738
South Boston, VA 24592
888/456-7837
www.gloster.com

Tidewater Workshop
1515 Grant St.
Egg Harbor, NJ 08215
800/666-8433
www.tidewaterworkshop.com

Tropitone Furniture Co.
5 Marconi
Irvine, CA 92618
949/951-2010
www.tropitone.com

garden design stencil & landscape design notebook

Lee Valley Tools
P.O. Box 1780
Ogdensburg, NY 13669-6780
800/871-8158
www.leevalleytools.com

gazebos

Gazebo Junction, Inc.
2627 Kaneville Ct.
Geneva, IL 60134
800/966-9261
www.gazebojunction.com

Vixen Hill Manufacturing Co.
Main St.
Elverson, PA 19520
800/423-2766
www.vixenhill.com

greenhouses

Santa Barbara Greenhouses
721 Richmond Ave.
Oxnard, CA 93030
800/544-5276
www.sbgreenhouse.com

Sundance Supply
P.O. Box 225
Olga, WA 98279
800/776-2534
www.sundancesupply.com

hammocks and swings

101 Hammocks
512/233-6524
www.101hammocks.com

Chairs of the Sky and Air
3525 Del Mar Heights
San Diego, CA 92130
800/488-2756
www.chairsoftheskyandair.com

Golden Hammocks
2220 Division St.
Waite Park, MN 56387
320/685-7653
www.goldenhammocks.com

Nags Head Hammocks
Milepost 9 Hwy. 158
Nags Head, NC 27959
800/344-6433
www.nagshead.com

Sky Chairs
828 Pearl St.
Boulder, CO 80302
800/759-8759
www.skychairs.com

lighting

Armadilla Wax Works, Inc.
2651 N. Industrial Way
Prescott Valley, AZ 86314
800/247-6045
www.waccents.com

Buy-Solar.com
73 Glenwood Ave.
Demarest, NJ 07527
800/837-6527

Intermatic, Inc.
Intermatic Plaza
Spring Grove, IL 60081-9698
800/492-2289

Lorijane Studio
118 B S. Acacia Ave.
Solana Beach, CA 92075
info@lorijane.com
www.lorijane.com

Stone Manor Lighting
9612 Porterdale Rd.
Malibu, CA 90265
888/534-0544
www.stonemanorlighting.com

mosquito netting

Barre Army/Navy Store
955 N. Main St.
Barre, VT 05641
800/448-7965
www.vtarmynavy.com/bugstuff.htm

motorized awnings

General Awning & Fabric
160-6660 Greybar Rd.
Richmond, BC Canada V6W 1H9
888/693-8833
www.generalawning.com

Betterliving Patio Rooms
926 Highway 72 E
Athens, AL 35611
800/977-4151
www.blpatiorooms.com

outdoor showers
Comfort House
189-V Frelinghuysen Ave.
Newark, NJ 07114-1595
800/359-7701
www.comforthouse.com

Specialty Pool Products, Inc.
110 Main St.
Broad Brook, CT 06016-0388
800/983-7665
www.poolproducts.com

recycled materials
ENVIROFORM Recycled Products, Inc.
28 Seeley Rd.
Geneva, NY 14456
800/789-1819
www.enviroform.com

QuickBrick
U.S. Rubber Recycling, Inc.
2225 Via Cerro, Unit B
Riverside, CA 92509
888/473-8453
www.usrubber.com

reed and bamboo matting
Bamboo Hardwoods
6402 Roosevelt Way NE
Seattle, WA 98115-6619
206/529-0978
www.bamboohardwoods.com

Cane & Basket Supply Co.
1283 South Cochran Ave.
Los Angeles, CA 90019
323/939-9644
www.canebasket.com

Connecticut Cane and Reed Co.
Box 762
Manchester, CT 06045
800/227-8498
www.caneandreed.com

structures
Arboria
LWO Corp.
P.O. Box 17125
Portland, OR 97217
503/286-5372
www.arboria.com

Archadeck U.S. Structures, Inc.
2112 W. Laburnum Ave., Suite 100
Richmond, VA 23227
800/722-4668
www.archadeck.com

Bloomsbury Market
403 S. Cedar Lake Road
Bryn Mawr, MN 55405
800/999-2411
www.bloomsburymkt.com

Trellis Structures
60 River St.
Beverly, MA 01915
888/285-4624
www.trellisstructures.com

Walpole Woodworkers
767 East St., Route 27
Walpole, MA 02081
800/343-6948
www.walpolewoodworkers.com

wind chimes & wind art
Imagine That! Windchimes
240 Curnutt Lane
Ten Mile, TN 37880
423/334-4629
www.imaginethatchimes.com

Music in the Wind
P.O. Box 812
Silverton, OR 97381
877/946-3687
www.musicinthewind.com

Toland Enterprises
1750 South Lane
Mandeville, LA 70471
888/933-5620
www.tolandnet.com

Wind & Weather
1200 N. Main St.
Fort Bragg, CA 95437
800/922-9463
www.windandweather.com

wooden swings, benches, & gliders
The Cedar Store
1620 Rt. 8
Glenshaw, PA 15116
888/293-2339
www.cedarstore.com

Creative Woodworking
7261 Highway 43 S.
Spruce Pine, AL 35585
888/225-2029
www.oakswings.com

Plow & Hearth
P.O. Box 6000
Madison, VA 22727-1600
800/627-1712
www.plowhearth.com

usda plant hardiness zone maps

These maps of climate zones can help you select plants for your garden that will survive a typical winter in your region. The United States Department of Agriculture (USDA) developed the map for North America, basing the zones on the lowest recorded temperatures. On a scale of 1 to 11, Zone 1 is the coldest area and Zone 11 is the warmest.

Plants are classified in zones by the coldest temperature they can endure. For example, plants hardy to Zone 6 survive where winter temperatures drop to −10° F. Those hardy to Zone 8 would die long before it's that cold. These plants may grow in colder regions but must be replaced each year. Plants rated for a range of hardiness zones can usually survive winter in the coldest region, as well as tolerate the summer heat of the warmest one.

To find your hardiness zone, note the approximate location of your community on the map; then match the color marking that area to the key.

Make sure your plants will flourish in the weather in your area. Consult the last spring frost map, the first autumn frost map, and detailed state–specific hardiness maps at **www.bhg.com/bkzonemaps**

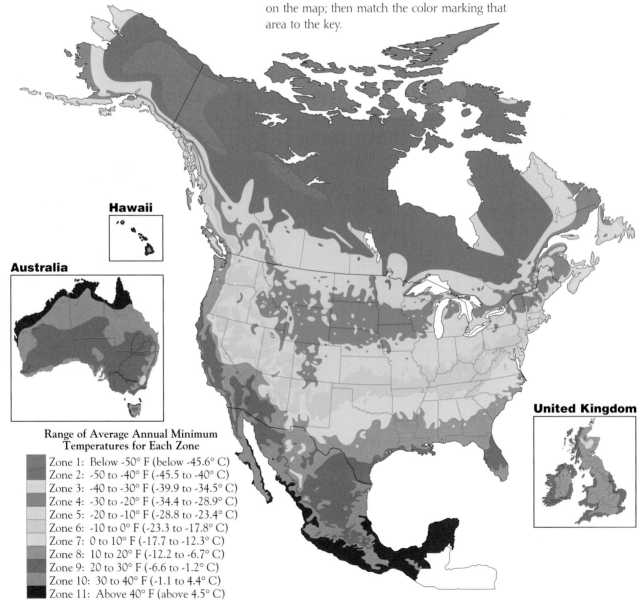

Hawaii

Australia

United Kingdom

Range of Average Annual Minimum Temperatures for Each Zone

Zone 1: Below -50° F (below -45.6° C)
Zone 2: -50 to -40° F (-45.5 to -40° C)
Zone 3: -40 to -30° F (-39.9 to -34.5° C)
Zone 4: -30 to -20° F (-34.4 to -28.9° C)
Zone 5: -20 to -10° F (-28.8 to -23.4° C)
Zone 6: -10 to 0° F (-23.3 to -17.8° C)
Zone 7: 0 to 10° F (-17.7 to -12.3° C)
Zone 8: 10 to 20° F (-12.2 to -6.7° C)
Zone 9: 20 to 30° F (-6.6 to -1.2° C)
Zone 10: 30 to 40° F (-1.1 to 4.4° C)
Zone 11: Above 40° F (above 4.5° C)

index

index

index

index

index

r–s

Railings, 114, 134
Rain-chain, *283*
Raised bed, *80-81*, 112
Ramada, defined, 61
Rambler roses, *204, 205*
Recirculating fountain. *See* Fountain
Recycled materials, 15, 167
   concrete as bench, 172–173
   fencing, 48–49
   for edging, 167
   glass for flooring, *76-77*
   **junk mail and newspaper for
      papier-mâché, 274–275**
   tire planter, *242-243*
   **window frame, trellis
      from, 212–213**
   windows as garden house, *184-185*
Red cedar structure, *30-31*
Redwood, 89, 109, 118
   and cedar gazebo, *124-125*
   bender board, 122
   deck, *142-143*
   lanterns, 256–257
Reed matting, *152*
Reinforcing rod, as anchor, 203
Rerod, *221*
Reservoir, for fountain, *289*
Retaining wall, 15, 56, 82, 112
Retractable awning, *98, 99*
Rhododendron, 45
River rock, *76-77, 132-133, 167*
Rock
   crushed, 59
   fountain, *287*
   hollowed out for birdbath, *196*
   lava, *76-77*
   with millstone fountain, 132–133
Romantic garden style, 32–35
Roof
   arched, for pergola, 116–117
   scrap-metal mesh, *105*

slatted, *97*
   See also Ceilings
Room, outdoor, 10–13, 103, 128–157
   bathing, 154–157
   deck, 134-139
   dining, 144–147
   furnishings for, 170–179
   gazebo, multipurpose, 124–125
   living, 142–143
   meditation, *150-153*
   patio, 130–133
   rooftop, 140–141
   sleeping, 148–149
Rose, 25, 33, *96-97*, 103, *120*
   and trellises, 204–205
   climbing, 34, 111, 122, 131, 157, 180,
      188, 234
   for tabletop fountain, 252
   groundcover, 'Flower Carpet', 112
   miniature for tire planter, 243
   petals for bathing, 157
   red 'Dortmund', *210-211*
   shrub, 105
   white 'Alba', *210-211*
Rosemary, 157, 223
Rot, wood, checking for, 139
Rug, checkerboard, 138–139
Rustic
   garden style, 28–31
   plant markers, 276–277
   shower room, *154-155*
Safety tips, lighting, 250, 253
Sage, 157, 222-223
Salvaged material
   fence from, *83*
   garden house from, *184-187*
   satellite-dish, 61
   **window frame as trellis,
      210–211**
   See also Recycled materials
Santolina topiaries, *37*
Sasaella, dwarf bamboo, 46

Scarecrow, *272-273*
Scotch
   broom, 112
   moss, 34
Scrap-metal mesh roof, *105*
Screen
   bamboo, *Fastuosa* spp., 46
   fabric, hanging, 267
   garden, 67
   lattice, 92–93
Sculpture
   arbor as, *105*
   papier-mâché, 274–275
   wind art, 278–279
Sea-glass lantern, 262–263
Seating, *135*, 159
   Adirondack chair, 176–177
   concrete bench, 172–173
   for meditation room, 152
   hanging chairs, *136-137*
   options, 147, 150–151
Sedum, 39, 78, 166, *240*
Seeder, vintage, as planter, 229
**Seedlings, protecting with cloche,
   194–195**
Sempervivum, 39
Setcreasea, 41
Shade, 17
   dwarf mondo grass for, *32-33*
   outdoor structures for, 130
Shades, for string lights, 253
Shallow bowl planter, 240–241
Shed, *36*
   amenities for, 191
   garden, 188–191
   multi-purpose, *188, 189*
   tiny, for tool storage, 182–183
Shells, for edging, 166
Shelter, garden, 102–127
Shelves, in garden house, *187*
Shorea, 24, 43, *96*
Shower, outdoor, *154-155*

index

index

metric conversions

u.s. units to metric equivalents

to convert from	multiply by	to get
Inches	25.400	Millimeters
Inches	2.540	Centimeters
Feet	30.480	Centimeters
Feet	0.3048	Meters
Yards	0.9144	Meters
Square inches	6.4516	Square centimeters
Square feet	0.0929	Square meters
Square yards	0.8361	Square meters
Acres	0.4047	Hectares
Cubic inches	16.387	Cubic centimeters
Cubic feet	0.0283	Cubic meters
Cubic feet	28.316	Liters
Cubic yards	0.7646	Cubic meters
Cubic yards	764.550	Liters

To convert from degrees Celsius (C) to degrees Fahrenheit (F), multiply by $\frac{9}{5}$, then add 32.

metric units to u.s. equivalents

to convert from	multiply by	to get
Millimeters	0.0394	Inches
Centimeters	0.3937	Inches
Centimeters	0.0328	Feet
Meters	3.2808	Feet
Meters	1.0936	Yards
Square centimeters	0.1550	Square inches
Square meters	10.764	Square feet
Square meters	1.1960	Square yards
Hectares	2.4711	Acres
Cubic centimeters	0.0610	Cubic inches
Cubic meters	35.315	Cubic feet
Liters	0.0353	Cubic feet
Cubic meters	1.308	Cubic yards
Liters	0.0013	Cubic yards

To convert from degrees Fahrenheit (F) to degrees Celsius (C), first subtract 32, then multiply by $\frac{5}{9}$.